LIBERAL EDUCATION
AND
VALUE RELATIVISM

A Guide to Today's B.A.

Patrick Malcolmson
Richard Myers
Colin O'Connell

University Press of America, Inc.
Lanham • New York • London

Copyright © 1996 by
University Press of America,® Inc.
4720 Boston Way
Lanham, Maryland 20706

3 Henrietta Street
London, WC2E 8LU England

Library of Congress Cataloging-in-Publication Data

Malcolmson, Patrick.
Liberal education and value relativism : a guide to today's B.A. /
Patrick Malcolmson, Richard Myers, Colin O'Connell.
p.   cm.
Includes bibliographical references.
1. Education, Humanistic--United States. 2. Bachelor of arts degree--
United States. 3. Ethical relativism. 4. Cultural relativism--United
States. 5. Education, Higher--United States--Curricula. 1. Myers,
Richard. II. O'Connell, Colin. III. Title.
LC1023.M35   1996   370.11'4--dc20   96-13032   CIP

ISBN 0-7618-0336-X (cloth: alk. ppr.)
ISBN 0-7618-0337-8 (pbk: alk. ppr.)

Contents

Foreword

I never liked university very much. In fact, I still find it hard to get nostalgic about sitting in u-shaped desks or writing essays about historical materialism.

Part of my dislike may have had something to do with the scale of my alma mater York University. Its sprawling campus was inspired by California architecture and a lust for concrete. Big and alien, York seemed far removed from the geographic realities of everyday life as well as the rich farmland it had covered up.

My distrust of university and its conceits was also ideologically rooted. While a student I was an earnest Christian-Marxist, the kind that couldn't quaff a beer without thinking how blue collar workers were being taxed to subsidize my studies. I was indeed privileged and felt undeserving of it.

I chose to attend university to study my passion Latin American history. I had no illusions about preparing myself for a career because the thoughts of Sarmiento, Pancho Villa and Che Guervara lent themselves more to revolutionary endeavors than a nine-to-five job. But while I despaired of the betrayals of the Mexican Revolution and the quartering of Tupac Amaru, my peers seemed driven by hopeful dreams of upward mobility.

I now realize that my unease with academic studies and the ambitions of my peers also reflected a growing confusion about the purpose of university itself. I entered the ivory tower at a time when the institution's phenomenal growth and popularity had already caused it to lose sight of its true purpose. Students like myself didn't understand this at the time, or really appreciate how much the idea of a liberal education had been sacrificed to the ends of commerce and political fashion.

Few books have explored these themes for prospective students as directly and clearly as this one. It has been written by teachers concerned about conserving what is most valuable about a university. It begins by reminding aspiring students that a liberal education is not essentially about "Western civilization," "critical thinking," or "job preparation." A proper education shouldn't train people to be consumers, technicians or ideologues but rather challenge them to be noble, good and thoughtful human beings. It seeks to give its participants as the Aztecs might say, "a wise countenance and stout heart." In this regard the authors observe that a true liberal education is an expensive luxury and probably one of "incomparable worth."

But it is also a luxury being undermined by dogmas and trends that have little respect for the pursuit of truth. Perhaps the greatest threat to liberal education is one of the university's greatest exports: value relativism. This popular doctrine holds that all judgements are subjective, that all ideas are merely opinions and that all opinions carry the same weight. Not surprisingly, it leads to the creation of a "relativist curriculum" – one that resembles a great shopping mall of studies where "there is no synoptic view, no whole perspective, no permanent questions, no perennial issues, no fundamental human concerns." When universities lose sight of the highest goal – a fully developed human being – they can't help but treat students simply as consumers who know already what they need to learn.

This prostitution of purpose to businesslike interests and political goals makes a liberal education harder and harder to get. For the disappearance of essential and basic studies from most universities – the true core of a liberal education – really means the end of learning that would inform civil judgement about what matters and what doesn't.

In criticizing these trends and their symptoms (such as the poverty of specialization, deconstructionism and political correctness) the authors ably defend common standards and the quest for universal truths. Obtaining a liberal education is hard work, they say, but pursuing ideas of value and their fate in the world is still worth spending four years of one's life and many thousands of dollars.

My long university years were not wasted. Many of the truths I learned about democratic society, economics and human behavior there continue to inform my journalism and public life. And though I wouldn't care to repeat the experience (a liberal education can be achieved outside of ivory towers), I still value its true purpose, and recommend this book as an antidote to muddled thinking and the infectious aimlessness of campus life.

Andrew Nikiforuk

Preface

The authors' intention is to provide prospective university students with a clear description of the nature and purpose of liberal education, as we understand it. This book is not meant to be a historical work. Our standards are drawn not from an account of what the university was in some mythical golden age, but from our attempt to think through the first principles of liberal education.

Though the questions we deal with are complex ones, we have tried, for the sake of our audience, to present them as simply as possible. It may be that more experienced readers, especially our fellow educators, will find some of it too simplified, simplistic, or polemical. Those who are not value relativists might even go so far as to maintain that we are wrong! We welcome healthy debate on the topics we have introduced, and, in the spirit of Socratic dialectic, we encourage those who disagree with us to join the discussion by writing books of their own.

Patrick Malcolmson
Richard Myers
Colin O'Connell

Acknowledgments

The authors would like to acknowledge the contributions made by the following people whose comments, criticisms, and suggestions enabled us to make substantial improvements to our text: Michael Alexander, Rodney Boyd, Jo-Anne Brant, Robert Chaulk, David Conrad, Lorne Dawson, Beth Gordon, Antonio and Peggy Gualtieri, Joseph Knippenberg, John Kohler, Borys Kowalski, Keith and Laura Morgan, Colin Pearce, Anne Pearson, David and Els Salisbury, Walter Schultz, William Sweet, Gérard Vallée, Mark Vorobej, and Darcy Wudel. We would like to thank them for helping us to articulate our case more clearly, even when their own views diverged significantly from those expressed in this book.

Introduction

Each September, hundreds of thousands of young men and women enroll in the Bachelor of Arts programs in North America's many colleges and universities. It is astonishing how few first year students are able to articulate a clear understanding of what they hope to get from a B.A., and why the liberal arts are worth studying. Most of them sense that an education in arts will somehow "broaden" them, but would find it difficult to say how. Presumably, they think that someone will explain this once their studies begin.

Unfortunately, such an expectation is unrealistic. Most colleges and universities do virtually nothing to promote a better understanding of the ultimate aims and objectives of a liberal arts education. They do invest a great deal of time, money, and effort in organizing elaborate "orientation" programs for their incoming students. Yet these programs deal exclusively with practical matters like how to register, where to find the library, and what to do if you want to change roommates. Usually there is some form of "course counselling" available during the registration process, but this tends to be nothing more than a means of ensuring that the student's schedule of courses satisfies the school's curricular requirements. Once classes begin, individual professors might say a few words about why their particular subject is worth studying (although it is surprising how many do not). Yet nobody takes responsibility for talking to students about their education as a whole. This leaves new students totally bereft of intellectual guidance as they try to figure out what they should take, how to tell a good course from a bad one, and how to make of their education the most broadening experience possible.

This book is designed to fill that gap. It has been prepared by three professors who teach undergraduate arts courses. Our intention is to explain the primary nature and purpose of the B.A., and to forewarn students about some of the problems that now beset most B.A. programs. In the first chapter, we attempt to explain what the deepest objectives of an arts education are and why one should seriously consider pursuing such an education. This, we hope, will give students a better sense of what they should be looking for in their courses.

To describe what one should be looking for inevitably entails describing what one should avoid. It is an unfortunate fact that most of today's arts programs lack coherence and vision. Our colleges and universities rarely make anything more than a feeble attempt at defining some core set of ideas and questions that any truly educated person should have reflected on. In Chapters II and III, we attempt to explain the root causes of this situation. We also try to introduce the reader to some of the most problematic trends in the contemporary university.

In our fourth and final chapter, we survey the various fields of study available to B.A. students and discuss how each might or might not contribute to the student's pursuit of a liberal education. This will enable students to choose their courses in a more informed manner and so improve their chances of obtaining the best liberal education available to them.

Chapter I

The Idea Of A Liberal Education

What is the purpose of doing an arts degree? Those who are supposed to know about such things have a simple answer for you. When confronted with this question, university presidents and professors will inevitably tell you that the point of doing a B.A. is to get a "liberal education." This is, in fact, a fine answer. But what precisely does it mean? Here we run into trouble.

"Liberal education" is actually quite an old term – probably older than the very idea of the university. But did you ever notice how the older some ideas get, the more we take them for granted, and the less we actually understand them? They become like old coins with the faces rubbed off. This is pretty much what has happened with the idea of liberal education. With the passing of time, it has degenerated into a cliché or a platitude, its meaning so debased that it is now used to signify almost anything.

Liberal Education: Three Inadequate Definitions

The three most common definitions of liberal education in today's university are: liberal education as general education in the arts; liberal education as "critical thinking"; and liberal education as "Western civilization." None of these definitions is wholly wrong; yet none of them captures the fundamental idea of a liberal education.

Probably the most common, and certainly the most superficial definition of liberal education is "general education in those subjects which traditionally constitute the liberal arts." In other words, if you take a general program in arts, you automatically get a liberal education.

What makes this definition popular is that it simplifies things so nicely, both for students and for those who run the university. It frees the latter from any tough decisions about what should be taught and whether or not certain courses should be required. And it leaves the students free to take whatever courses they feel like, without suffering any doubts about the quality of their education.

The problem, however, is that this definition lacks substance because it is purely formal. It assumes that all the courses now taught in arts programs are equally valuable in terms of promoting liberal education. Such an assumption is simply untenable. In the first place, universities offer many courses which have little to do with liberal education. Knowing how to operate computers is a useful thing, but it is difficult to see how "Introduction to Computer Literacy" contributes to liberal education. Moreover, as we shall explain in Chapter III, even in fields which have traditionally been thought to constitute the backbone of liberal education (fields such as literature or philosophy) many of today's instructors see the aim of their courses as something other than liberal education. Some regard their mission to be the advancement of certain political ideals, for instance, while others believe their task is to train specialized researchers.

The second definition of liberal education – liberal education as critical thinking – suffers from a similar failure to specify the substance of the concept. This definition appeals to those who wish to play up the economic utility of the B.A. In talking about education, these people focus on the activity of learning and thinking. For them, the primary objective of an arts education is the acquisition of the intellectual skills one needs to be successful in the modern economy – skills in oral and written communication, analytical thinking, and so on. Subject matter is thought to be of less importance; those taking this view argue that it doesn't make much difference what you study – Russian history, Italian poetry – as long as in doing so you learn to think about your subject in a critical way and to communicate your thoughts effectively.

No sensible person could argue with the idea that a good education should teach people to think critically. But does it really makes sense to say that subject matter is nothing more than grist for the critical thinking mill? Thought through to its logical, but absurd conclusion, this definition of liberal education would suggest that thinking critically about who will win the Super Bowl might be as valid a topic of university study as anything else. Surely liberal education is something more than that.

There is an influential group of people who try to define liberal education in a way that does entail a very specific subject matter. These people see liberal education as a general introduction to the history of Western culture and civilization. Although there is an element of truth to this view, it is ultimately neither accurate nor sufficient.

The problem with defining liberal education as "Western Civ" is that it makes the touchstone for deciding what we study the ethnic origin of topics rather than their inherent importance: if it's Western, we study it, and if not, we don't. On the one hand, such a definition is too broad. Putting things in the curriculum because they are part of Western civilization would logically lead us to the study of Roman law, the divine right of kings, and the history of Christmas trees, toilets, and the automobile. On the other hand, this definition is in a sense too narrow, for it would automatically exclude important literature and ideas that come from non-Western sources.

Any liberally educated person should certainly be familiar with the major ideas and trends in Western civilization – democracy, rationalism, romanticism, feminism, modern natural science, separation of church and state, and so on. But the question we must ask ourselves is whether we need to know about these things because they are "Western" or because they are important to how we live our lives. Common sense tells us that it is the latter. And this points to a more satisfactory understanding of what liberal education really means.

The Aim of Liberal Education

Let us start from the beginning. A liberal education is a particular kind of education. Vocational education is the kind of education necessary to engage in work. Professional education is for the purpose of practising a particular profession such as law or medicine. We know what "vocation" and "profession" mean, and hence know what those kinds of education are. What, then, does the word "liberal" mean in this context?

The English adjective "liberal" is derived from the Latin *liber* which means "free." Liberal education is thus the kind of education that is fitting for a free human being, or, alternatively, the sort of education that will free one from the slavishness of ignorance.

The fundamental premise of liberal education is that human freedom, in its fullest sense, is a function of our wisdom concerning those matters which are most central to how we live our lives. To illustrate the point, let us take as an example a person who has an obviously problematic view of life. What would you think of a man who truly believes that the only thing that counts in life is making as much money as possible, that love, family, friendship, and honor are all illusory or unimportant? Would you not have to say that his foolishness or lack of wisdom has led to a kind of enslavement, an enslavement to the pursuit of money? And is it not clear that in order to free himself from that enslavement, that person would need to do a lot more thinking about some of life's great questions? That is exactly what liberal education means. *Liberal education is a sustained and open-minded examination of the deepest questions of human existence, an examination that is meant to free us of our prejudices in such matters.*

Everyone agrees that prejudices are a bad thing. The problem, however, is that human beings have a tendency to think that it is only other people who have prejudices, that they themselves are both sensible and open-minded. We concede that the man who thinks that money is the only thing that counts is caught in a foolish prejudice; but we tend to see our own views as eminently reasonable. Liberal education begins with the hypothesis that everything we believe might, in fact, turn out to be nothing more than a foolish prejudice. Its aim is therefore to test our opinions about life before the bar of reason, subjecting each of them to careful rational scrutiny.

As far as we know, the founder of liberal education, in this sense, was a man named Socrates. Socrates lived in Ancient Greece about 2,500 years ago. He is best known for two claims. The first of these is that his wisdom consisted of a knowledge of his own ignorance. The second claim is "the unexamined life is not worth living."

To explain the first of these statements, it is useful to recount a famous story about Socrates. In Ancient Greece, the temple at Delphi had an oracle which was reputed to know everything, even the future. The Delphic oracle once declared that no one was wiser than Socrates. When Socrates heard about this claim, he modestly assumed that the oracle must have been mistaken, for he thought that his own city had many people who were far wiser than he. In order to refute the oracle, Socrates went to talk to some of the most famous politicians, poets, and craftsmen of Athens. His plan was to show that they knew much about many important matters, matters about which he himself knew nothing at all. In talking to these people, however, Socrates soon found that they did not really know anything about the matters in which they were supposed to be experts. The politicians, for example, were supposed to know what justice is. Yet Socrates found that everytime he asked them to define justice, the definitions they offered were easily shown to be flawed. After extensive conversations with such people, Socrates came to the conclusion that he was, in fact, the wisest of human beings. For while others claimed to know the truth about things, but clearly did not, he at least was not caught in the trap of thinking he knew more than he did.

The story about the Delphic oracle also helps us to understand Socrates' second statement – "the unexamined life is not worth living." In the course of his discussions with the poets, artisans, and politicians, Socrates came to realize that all of these people were building their entire lives on opinions which they had never examined adequately. The politicians devoted themselves to the cause of justice, but could not explain what justice is. The poets spent their lives writing about love, but could not properly define it. It soon occurred to Socrates that all human beings base their lives on certain opinions about what is good and what is bad, what is noble and what is base, what is honourable and what is dishonourable, but that almost no one ever examines those opinions rigorously. Our opinions on these matters are therefore little more than prejudices, so that our lives are like a house of cards, with everything resting on extremely shaky foundations. It was this insight that led Socrates to the conclusion that the unexamined life is not worth living. For if we are to lead good and happy lives, we need to examine as carefully as possible all those opinions which will serve as the foundation for the way we live.

The Questions of Liberal Education

The central question in liberal education is the question of the good life: what is the good life for human beings as such? This is the question that dominated Socrates' quest for wisdom. And though subsequent thinkers have approached the question in dramatically different ways, it has always remained *the* crucial question of liberal education.

This should come as no surprise. The philosopher Aristotle began his famous book on ethics with the observation that all human action seems to aim at some good. He did not mean that we are always trying to do good for others or to be good in an ethical sense. He meant rather that we are always acting on the basis of some belief about what is good. One thus seeks money, fame, power, pleasure, and other such things in the belief that they are good things to possess. What we most need to think about, then, is our conception of what is good for human beings in general. In other words, we need to reflect upon our idea of what the best human life would be like, what good things would characterize it, and what evils it would be free from.

The paramount importance of this question of the human good should be self-evident. However little we may be aware of it, everything we do as human beings is done with some idea of the good in mind. The saint sacrifices her life in the belief that this is the best life for a human being. The petty criminal steals in the belief that he is getting the good things for himself. Human beings act on the basis of incredibly diverse opinions about what is good. But there is no getting around the fact that they always act with some idea of the good in mind.

There is perhaps no mistake more regrettable than a mistake concerning what the good is; for without a clear understanding of that idea, how could we ever make prudent decisions in our basic life-choices? Do I want to devote myself to my religion? Do I want to devote myself to personal pleasure? Do I want to have a family? Should I fight for my country if it goes to war?

People are often reluctant to face up to the question of the human good. They find it easier to persuade themselves that one can muddle through such problems on the basis of "common sense." Though they cannot say exactly what the good life is, they know that it isn't simply the pursuit of money. To simplify matters, they are inclined to take the view that the good life is happiness, and happiness is whatever makes you feel good.

But this view is totally unsatisfactory. In the first place, you can never understand happiness simply by trying to gauge your "feelings." Indeed, it should be obvious that, more often than not, our feelings actually mislead us. We may feel one way about something Saturday night, but then feel very differently about it Sunday morning. A reasonable approach to happiness thus depends on our ability to act in accordance with principles, and our capacity to choose sound principles, which are not merely a reflection of transitory "feelings," depends almost entirely on the care with which we have thought about what happiness means for human beings .

Yet even this is not satisfactory. Is it really adequate to say that the good life consists in the pursuit of happiness? Is it not true that there are sometimes things we have to do, even though we know they are unpleasant and make us unhappy? This is a reflection of the fact that human beings are not simply concerned with their own happiness; they are also concerned with what we may call "the noble."

To define the noble in a precise way is not easy, but we all have a general sense of what the term signifies. Noble deeds are deeds which are worth doing, even at great cost to our happiness, because they are intrinsically right, because they are beautiful, or because they somehow capture and express what we sense is the higher side of human existence. A good example would be the sacrifices that human beings sometimes make for family, friends, or country in an emergency or at time of war.

But our sense of the noble is not something that emerges only in the extreme case. On the contrary, one can say that it permeates every aspect of our lives. In almost everything we think, do, and desire, we are dominated by a need to conform to standards which reflect our concern with the noble. Think, for example, how important it is to you and your friends to look, sound, and act in a way that will be perceived as "cool," or at least to avoid looking, sounding, or acting like a "jerk," a "geek," or whatever the equivalent expression might be in your particular circles. This is in fact a common expression (at a somewhat superficial level) of the human concern with the noble.

Human beings differ from animals in that it is not enough for us to satisfy our bodily needs. We seek something in addition, something higher. This fact becomes obvious when you think about the manner in which we treat even those physiological needs that we have in common with the animals – food, drink, and sex. Notice, for example, the degree to which human sexuality is complicated by all kinds of demands, hopes and expectations that are utterly foreign to animals. We feel a need for sexual activity, but we want our sexual relations to take place with someone who is attractive in both body and soul. Usually we even want it to be with someone we love and who loves us in return. Animals know nothing of this. As Jean-Jacques Rousseau pointed out, an animal will satisfy its sexual needs with the first thing that comes along, big or small. By the same token, animals satisfy their hunger by eating whatever they find, as long as it accords with their instincts. Human beings, on the other hand, are not satisfied merely to eat; they prefer to dine, to eat nobly, satisfying their hunger with nicely prepared food shared with pleasant company.

But the human concern with the noble is more than just a way of dressing up our physiological needs. Whether we realize it or not, it pervades almost everything we do and believe – what we think is a proper way to live, which human qualities are admirable, which actions are worth emulating, and which kind of human beings deserve our love or respect.

To understand the human good, then, we must give the most careful consideration to a number of important questions. For example, what is pleasure? Is there a hierarchy of pleasures? Are some good and others bad? If so, how do we rank them? What is noble? Are there some things which seem noble but are not? Are there others which do not seem noble but are? Is there a tension between the noble and the pleasant? If so, how do we settle conflicts between the two?

Our search for wisdom about the good leads to a concern with a number of other questions. One of these focuses on what the ancient Greeks called *arete* – "virtue" or "human excellence." What are the noble qualities that we admire in human beings, and seek to possess ourselves? Courage?

Prudence? Justice? Compassion? Piety? How do we recognize and define these qualities? And how do we apply them in particular cases? Which virtues are most important? How do we acquire them? Most importantly, what is the quality they all have in common? What is virtue in and of itself?

Many of you will think that these are questions that can be answered with common sense. This, unfortunately, is not the case. Let's take as an example one of the most important virtues – justice. We all admire people who are just, and want others to think of us as just in turn. But what exactly is justice? It seems that we know almost intuitively that certain things are just (keeping your word, for instance) and that others are unjust (stealing from small children). Once we go beyond obvious cases like those, however, the matter becomes quite murky. Is it just to give someone an edge in the competition for admission to a university on the basis of their race or sex when they are members of a group that has traditionally been disadvantaged? Intelligent people have serious disagreements over this. It is certainly true, as Aristotle once pointed out, that justice requires us to treat equals equally and unequals unequally. But then how do we determine what is equal and what is unequal? Equal or unequal in what sense? Do you measure people as individuals, or as members of groups? Is our identity as human beings primarily individual, or primarily collective?

These are difficult questions, and thinking about them will lead us into others still more difficult. To address such questions properly, we need much more than "common sense." We need to engage in serious and sustained reflection on the alternative points of view. That is not a simple matter, but self-respecting human beings cannot afford to ignore such questions just because they are complicated. After all, how you understand the crucial human virtue of justice will do infinitely more to define who you are as a person than the length or color of your hair or the kind of clothes you wear.

Another theme of liberal education is *eros*, or love. One of the ways in which we can begin to think about the question of what constitutes the best life for a human being – a life where one possesses the good things – is to reflect upon the nature of human desire and love. What is the meaning of this powerful sense of longing that is such a force in our lives? What do we love and why do we love it? Why do we long for romantic love? What is the meaning and proper role of our sexual longings? What about family life? Are there more than physiological differences between the sexes? If so, what significance do those differences have? What is the true and proper basis of friendship? Can there be true friendship between members of different sexes? And what about our broader attachments, the love of our city, our country, our fellow human beings? Are these natural, or are they merely illusions created by society?

Our *eros* is not directed merely towards physical things. Human beings are intensely curious creatures and they long to know all sorts of things. Moreover, they are capable of the more interesting emotion of wonder, a longing for knowledge about deeper and more important questions concerning things like the origin of the species, the nature of human genius, and the existence of God.

A lot can be known about a person simply by observing the sorts of things toward which their eros is directed. Have you thought about this in yourself? Such reflection often leads to some interesting discoveries. We frequently find that while we have difficulty articulating our ideas about what is most desirable, there is indeed a pattern to our longings. The self-knowledge that emerges from considering such patterns is central to a liberal education.

Connected with the question of love is another major theme or problem – death. What is the meaning of human mortality? What impact does the realization that we are finite beings have on the way we live? What happens to us after we die? Do we have immortal souls? Do we owe our existence to some divine being, and if so, what can we know about that being, and what difference does that make to the way we live?

Justice, love, God, death, friendship, community – these are themes and questions that touch the very core of our being. The task of a liberal education is both to enlighten us concerning these matters, and to inspire us to pursue the noble path.

The questions raised in a liberal education are not the kind that have simple, straightforward answers. Perhaps this is why people are so reluctant to come to grips with them. While it is possible to ignore these questions, however, one cannot avoid them; for even if we do not face up to them consciously, in every moment of our lives we act on the basis of some implicit answer to them. Liberal education therefore begins with an awareness of this puzzle: if we have not given life's great questions careful thought, then where did we get our answers from?

The Cave

The solution to this puzzle is presented most powerfully and most profoundly in one of the most famous passages in all of literature, Plato's Allegory of the Cave. At the beginning of Book VII of *The Republic*, when the character Socrates is describing to a young man named Glaucon how difficult it is for a human being to become truly wise, he makes his point by comparing our existence to that of prisoners in a dark, underground cavern:

"Liken our nature, in its education or lack of education, to the following condition. See human beings as though they were in an underground cave-like dwelling, with a long entrance opening to the light across the whole cave. They have been in it since childhood, with their legs and necks in fetters so that they are kept looking forward only, and are unable to turn their heads around because of the fetters. They have light from a fire burning above and far behind them. Above the prisoners, between them and the fire, is a road, along which see a wall, constructed like the partitions that puppet-masters set up in front of people and over which they display their puppets."

"I see," he said.

"Next see human beings carrying all sorts of objects along that wall, holding them above it – figures of men and other animals, made of stone, wood and all sorts of other materials. As is likely, some of those carrying the objects make sounds, and others are silent."

"It's a strange image you speak of," he said, "and strange prisoners."

"They're like us," I said. "For first of all, do you think such human beings would have seen anything either of themselves or of one another other than the shadows cast by the fire on the wall of the cave opposite them?"

"How could they have," he said, "if they had been forced to keep their heads motionless their whole lives."

"And what of the objects being carried along the wall. Wouldn't the same thing be true of them?"

"Of course."

"If, then, they were able to discuss things with one another, don't you believe that they would call what they see the objects themselves?"

"Necessarily."

"And what if the prison also had an echo from the opposite wall? Whenever one of those going by should utter a cry, do you think they would believe the thing crying out to be anything other than the shadow?"

"No, by Zeus, I don't," he said.

"Then such human beings would undoubtedly hold the truth to be nothing other than the shadows of artificial things?" I said.

"Absolutely," he said.[1]

The general point of this strange vision is not hard to grasp. Socrates is suggesting that though we do not realize it, our minds are utterly enslaved to certain authoritative opinions. We believe we are free to think what we like, but this is actually true only in the sense that the prisoners in the cave are free to think what they like about the shadows on the wall which they are forced to watch, and which, because they have never seen anything else, they mistake for real things. The Allegory of the Cave thus suggests that we are in a sense victims of a kind of propaganda. Our opinions about most things in life appear to be freely chosen, but in reality, we embrace whatever opinions dominate our world. For having no real experience of any alternatives, we have a tendency to treat those opinions, many of which may be mistaken, as self-evident truths.

This will perhaps sound both abstract and far-fetched, but the force of Socrates' point becomes evident if you think about some concrete examples. Did you ever notice how those whose parents are staunch supporters of a particular political party often end up supporting the same party as their parents? Or think of religion. We all know that people born in Islamic countries tend to embrace the Islamic faith, while those born in Christian lands tend to become Christians (at least nominally).

Certainly these people are free to "choose" to adopt a different faith, but they rarely do. Sometimes this is because the authority of the dominant opinion in their time and place intellectually intimidates them. More frequently (and more dangerously), this is because years of experience with one's own faith make any other possibility seem absurd. Now Socrates is suggesting that this type of enslavement characterizes our opinions on *all* of the most important questions in life, that our thinking about the good and the noble, about love, justice, and friendship, is stifled, if not fully stunted, by our enslavement to the authority of our cave. Our "society," our "culture," our political regime – all of these things constitute a worldview whose authority over us is virtually absolute, precisely because it is the only one we know. And no matter how open we think we are to other views, no matter how much diversity we believe we experience, we always see *everything* only from the perspective of our own cave.

You will probably be reluctant to accept that what Socrates is saying might be true of yourself. You might acknowledge that the Allegory of the Cave is perhaps an accurate description of certain "primitive" societies like Socrates' own (where many thought slavery was acceptable, for example, or believed that the sun was a god). *"But we are different,"* you say. *"Our society is a free society, based on enlightenment, science, and human rights. We have abolished superstition. We have freedom of thought, freedom of expression and freedom of religion. No one tells me what to think."* All of this is (or seems) quite true. But notice that nobody tells the prisoners in Socrates' cave what to think either. There is no need to. And that is why *they* insist, with the most absolute conviction, that their opinions are all freely chosen. Just like *you* do.

The Allegory of the Cave thus demonstrates most powerfully why liberal education is necessary. Human beings of necessity lead their lives on the basis of certain opinions about what is good, what is noble, what is just, and dozens of other such matters. But those opinions are almost never freely chosen. Because we have not investigated these matters for ourselves, we are prisoners of whatever opinions happen to be dominant among our family and friends or in our society at large. In Socratic terms, we are slaves of the puppet-masters in the cave, accepting uncritically whatever images they project on the wall in front of us.

Only a genuine liberal education can liberate us from such slavery. For as long as we remain uncritically attached to the authoritative ideas of our age, even those of us who try to be open-minded will never escape the chains of our cave. The questions we raise and the answers we propose will always miss the mark. We would be like a group of prisoners in the cave discussing whether the shadow that was just flashed on the wall was a beaver or a duck. Or, to vary the metaphor, we would be like a driver whose car is stuck in the snow. We rev our engines and our wheels spin furiously but we don't get anywhere.

For our thinking to be fruitful, we must somehow weaken the hold our cave has on us. That is precisely what liberal education is meant to do. Remember that in Socrates' description of it, the cave contains a long passageway that eventually leads out to the light of the sun. Outside of the cave, people can see things as they really are. By offering us a sustained and critical examination of the alternative answers to the most fundamental questions, including many alternatives that may at first strike us as absurd, immoral or just plain bizarre, liberal education shows us that much of what we believe may be nothing more than the prejudices of our time and place. This is the only way to get on the path out of the cave. Indeed, one might say that at its deepest level, liberal education may be defined as precisely that: *liberation* from the cave.

Conclusion

This, in brief, is the essence of liberal education, the highest, the noblest, and the most fully human form of education. Its final objective is the formation of thoughtful and civilized human beings. A genuine liberal education should make you a different person, by giving you new perspectives on the questions that ultimately define our humanity. And it should give you a life-long taste for the beautiful, the noble, the true, and the good. As such, liberal education is perhaps the greatest of luxuries in our modern world. It is a luxury in that, with no promise of any economic return, it costs a great deal of time and money; and, more importantly, it is a luxury in the sense that it is a prize of incomparable worth.

As we suggested in the *Introduction*, however, our colleges and universities are not as hospitable to liberal education as they should be. The three great trends which dominate the modern university – specialization, democratization, and politicization – now make it increasingly difficult for students to obtain a genuine liberal education. In order to enable you to understand what these trends are and how they affect university instruction, we shall discuss them in Chapter III. Before we turn to that discussion, however, it will be necessary to acquaint you with the powerful dogma that is ultimately at the root of those three trends, and that poses the deepest threat to liberal education – the doctrine of value relativism. This is the subject of Chapter II.

Chapter II

Value Relativism

The university began as an institution devoted to the ideal of liberal education outlined in Chapter I. Today's university is a quite different institution. Universities are now devoted primarily to meeting the economic and social needs of society, to producing the specialized experts in the human and non-human technologies necessary to our way of life. Vocational training and a devotion to technological progress are the modern university's defining characteristics. The philosophical questions that once formed the core of liberal education are treated as peripheral or secondary.

It is no wonder that the liberal arts have sunk to such a low place in the modern university; it would be cause for wonder if they did not continue sinking. For liberal education is now confronted with the following objection: *"What can liberal arts courses teach us about anything fundamentally important? These courses focus on philosophical discussions and fictional treatments of themes such as good and evil, love, beauty, friendship, justice, happiness and the like. But who is to say what is good or evil? Is beauty not in the eye of the beholder?*

And is happiness not a subjective emotional condition unique to each individual?"

This is the objection of the "value relativist." Value relativism is a doctrine that holds that all judgments of value are "subjective" in the sense that they are relative to the time, culture, or personality of the subject who makes them. Hindus see cows as sacred, for example, while most North Americans see cows as potential cheeseburgers. According to the value relativist, neither view is "true" in any objective sense. In fact, there is no such thing as truth – the world is merely a collection of equally arbitrary value judgments.

Because the doctrine of value relativism holds that there are no universally and permanently true answers to the great questions of human existence, it poses a direct and deadly challenge to the very possibility of liberal education. On the theoretical plane, relativism renders the quest for human wisdom pointless. And psychologically speaking, relativism creates the most debilitating teaching environment possible. For students are not inclined to pursue in any serious way questions for which they believe there are no true answers.

In the last chapter, we suggested that modern North Americans are perhaps every bit as imprisoned in a "cave" as were the ancient Greeks and other earlier peoples. You probably found it difficult to imagine how that could be so. In this chapter, you will find a concrete example of what we mean. We believe that value relativism, in its many different forms, casts one of the longest shadows in our cave. The idea that there is no good, no evil, no noble, no base, no virtue, no justice, in short, no "truth" about anything that is fundamentally important – this has become one of the great dogmas of our time.

In our first-year political science course at St. Thomas University, we ask how many of our students would agree with the proposition that judgments of value are never true, but are always relative to the time, place or personality of those making them.[2] It is astonishing how every year, in every class, almost every single student agrees with this proposition. (One wonders if a professor in Ancient Greece could have obtained such overwhelming consent to the proposition that the sun is really a god named Helios!) Yet what is even more striking than this nearly unanimous acceptance of the principles of value relativism is the inability of our students to defend those principles when we raise the simplest of objections. This, to us, is the sign of a quasi-religious dogma, an indication that today's youth are under the full control of the puppet-masters of our cave.

Relativism shapes much of our vision of the world, and, as we shall see in the next chapter, much of the contemporary university's vision of its mission. Because of the influence of value relativism, and because of its inherent incompatibility with liberal education, the quest for liberal education in our age must begin with a careful consideration of this doctrine. That is why in this second chapter, we turn to a brief critical examination of the common arguments made on behalf of the various forms of value relativism. Our intention is not to "refute" relativism, but to get you thinking critically about a doctrine you probably embrace without really thinking about it. This will permit you to decide for yourself whether liberal education, as we have described it, is possible and desirable.

Perspectivism: All Opinions Are Equal

Perhaps you have had the experience of having someone say to you in the course of a discussion or friendly argument that while they cannot prove you wrong, they consider what you have said to be "just your opinion" and they shall therefore continue to hold their opposing view. "*Everyone is entitled to their own opinion."* And *"who is to say which opinion is better than another?"* After all, *"we each have our own unique perspective,"* and *"everything is relative."*

This is the kind of relativism known as "perspectivism." Perspectivism holds that there is no such thing as objective truth because truth is relative to each individual. If I think something is just, then for me, it is. But it is not just in any objective way. If you believe the same thing is unjust, then it is, for you.

Perspectivism may provide a convenient way for people to agree to disagree and hence all get along nicely, but it is hardly the basis of a reasonable conversation. And one need only think briefly about perspectivism to see some rather obvious problems. First, consider the idea that whatever you say is "just your opinion." Yes, our views are usually expressed in the form of opinions, but we all know that opinions can be more or less reasonable depending on the kinds of arguments we can make to support them. Can we give good reasons for why we hold the opinion we do? Do we have evidence? Can we make a logically coherent argument? Almost no one is so silly as to assert that "this is my opinion and I am going to stick to it although I have no reasons for doing so." The very idea of an opinion, as opposed to a mere grunt of approval or of pain, implies the need to justify one's position with reasoned argument.

Secondly, the idea that something is good or bad simply because a person believes that it is good or bad, that it all depends on one's personal perspective, is more than a little problematic. Let us say, for example, that I assert that arsenic is good for one's health, and to prove my point, I eat some. My death from arsenic poisoning would demonstrate that my view was incorrect; and the fact that I believed arsenic to be good for me would not change the fact that arsenic is poisonous. Merely believing something is good does not make it so.

Perhaps the most comic aspect of the perspectivist argument is that it boils down to an argument for human infallibility. Whatever I say is good is good, and I can never be wrong. But is it not obvious that our opinions often change as we realize that our views are in fact mistaken? Last week I thought John was a nice guy. Then after he stole my wallet, I thought he was a terrible person. Obviously one of my opinions was wrong. So how can all opinions be equal?

Yet we are likely to hear the further argument that "*well ....* *everyone is entitled to their own opinion.*" At the very least, this expresses a fundamental principle of our liberal democratic regime, and perhaps an important moral truth about politics. For we are here speaking of the principle of toleration, and the doctrines of free speech and free thought. But there are two important points to note about this argument. First, it is irrelevant; for the fact that we are each entitled to hold our own opinion says *nothing at all* about the value of our opinions. We are entitled to hold wrong opinions – that the moon is made of green cheese, that Edmonton is the capital of Canada, or that Russia is the smallest country in the world.

Secondly, the right to hold and express different opinions in no way suggests that all opinions are necessarily of equal value. In fact, the assertion of such a right suggests the opposite. For we do not hold the view that the "opinion" that everyone has a right to free speech and free thought is only relatively true and hence no more or less right than the opinion that you must think whatever I command you to think. We believe that the opinion that free speech is a fundamental right is a true opinion, and that those who disagree – Stalinists or Nazis, for example – are wrong.

Emotivism – the Fact/Value Distinction

Almost no one holds to the idea of a simple individual relativism of the kind just described, at least not for very long. But value relativism is usually supported by a more sophisticated argument based on a doctrine called "emotivism." Emotivism turns upon a philosophical distinction between judgments of fact and judgments of value. The argument, simply stated, runs something like this: *"Facts are things that can be demonstrated or empirically tested and proven true. They can be validated by the scientific method. Values, on the other hand, are not things that can be rationally justified. They are really statements of our emotional preferences, albeit ones that we often attempt to rationalize after the fact. But they are derived from our emotions and not our reason. Whereas facts are "objective," values are merely "subjective." For they depend upon the emotional preferences or passions of the subject doing the valuing."*

What the emotivist is arguing is really quite simple: value judgments are at bottom statements of the emotional preference of the person making the judgment. Whether these value judgments concern questions of justice or questions of beauty, they are ultimately grounded in emotion, not reason. They are expressions of an emotive "ought" and not a rational "is." We can therefore speak about how much we do value things, but we cannot speak about how much we *ought* to value them.

This point can be illustrated with a simple example. Some people prefer chocolate ice cream to vanilla. One could say they value chocolate more highly than they value vanilla. Their values, in this regard, are based on their tastes, which is to say that they value things more that give them greater pleasure. Other people may prefer vanilla to chocolate for similar reasons. These two groups of people have different values, which are in turn the result of different tastes and preferences. We can observe the *fact* that their values differ; but we cannot say which *value* is superior. We cannot say that valuing chocolate more highly than vanilla (or vice versa) is either right or wrong.

When we use a trivial example like ice cream, the distinction between facts and values seems persuasive. But does the distinction seem equally persuasive when we move out of the realm of the trivial? Does the argument that all judgments of value are the result of personal tastes or subjective preferences hold up when we move into the realms of politics, morality, and art? Some have argued that it does. This position was stated with great clarity by the 17th century philosopher Thomas Hobbes:

> But whatsoever is the object of any man's appetite or desire, that is it which he for his part calls *good*; and the objects of his hate and aversion *evil; and of his contempt, vile and inconsiderable.* For these words of good, evil, and contemptible, are ever used with relation to the person that uses them: there being nothing simply and absolutely so.[3]

Hobbes is arguing that what we value is determined by our subjective preferences, our "appetites" and "aversions." Things are good or bad relative to the appetites and aversions of the person judging them. If I have a desire to be generous, then I will value generosity as a good thing. If you have a desire to be stingy, then you will value stinginess as a good thing. Neither generosity nor stinginess can be said to be right in a general or universal sense, for all value is relative to the subject doing the valuing.

Hobbes' emotivist position must be considered very carefully. One author whose work might help you to do so is C.S. Lewis. Some of you are perhaps familiar with his novels *The Chronicles of Narnia, Out of the Silent Planet,* or *The*

Screwtape Letters. Lewis also wrote a number of important books on philosophy and theology, amongst which is his famous essay *The Abolition of Man*. First published in 1943, this essay remains one of the most penetrating and devastating critiques of emotivism in popular literature.

Lewis asks his reader to consider the accuracy of emotivism as a description of how we make value judgments. Suppose we are viewing a waterfall, a scene of such natural beauty that we describe it as sublime. According to the emotivist theory of value, our value judgement is not based on an objective assessment of the value of the waterfall in terms of its beauty. It is merely a statement of our emotional condition, our feelings of pleasure or aversion, at the time we viewed the waterfall. Because the waterfall caused us to feel certain pleasant emotions, we hold it to be valuable. When we appear to be saying something important about the nature of things, all we are actually doing is saying something about our own emotional state. This is the emotivist explanation.

Lewis asks us to consider what this theory could mean. First off, when we say that the waterfall is sublime we are not, according to Lewis, giving a description of our own emotions. When one says something is beautiful, one is not saying "I have beautiful emotions." What emotion is one purportedly describing? If you ponder this question for a moment, you will see that the idea that we are merely projecting our own emotional preferences into or onto things is surely not straightforward.[4] For it is difficult to say which emotion we are describing.

But suppose one were to answer that this waterfall seems sublime because it fills you with a sense of awe and wonder. Your emotions of awe and wonder are then the basis of your value judgement that the waterfall is indeed sublime. But what causes you to feel those emotions? And what do you think of others who do not feel similar emotions? Is it reasonable to believe that they simply have a different set of emotional preferences than us? Or do we not think that they are missing out on something important, that they are, like those who are colour blind or tone deaf, "aesthetically impaired?"

Consider now an example of moral value. Suppose, instead of a waterfall, we are viewing the commission of an immoral act, say the vigorous beating of a small child by an angry adult. We grow angry immediately and perhaps intervene. Such beatings are unjust and immoral, we tell the adult, and they must stop – or else. The emotive theory of value would have us believe that our value judgement is, as in the case above, purely subjective. When we describe the beating as unjust, we are saying nothing about the action itself but only about our feelings as aroused by the sight of the beating. These feelings are purely subjective. Some of us may grow angry and describe the beating as immoral; others may not and continue merrily on their way. But is the injustice of the act dependent upon the feelings of others? Or is it not the case that there is in fact something wrong with human beings who do not feel the appropriate emotions at the sight of such obvious injustice? One might call these the morally impaired.

Today it has become platitudinous to say that beauty is in the eye of the beholder. But according to Lewis, the alternative view should be reconsidered: beauty is appreciated by those who have eyes to see and ears to hear. Similarly, justice and morality are not simply our preferences and interests. They involve our conforming with specific principles of duty and action. For if all value judgments are simply dependent upon the emotional preferences of the valuers, then justice, like beauty, is also in "the eye of the beholder." Does that seem reasonable to you?

Consider the political implications of such a position. If something is moral or just simply because a person believes it is so, how are we to tell when a person acts morally? One would be forced to conclude that all their actions are by definition moral and just simply because they conform to the person's preference. In other words, no one is ever unjust. And if one person's emotional preferences conflict with another's how are we to settle the dispute? It seems that we cannot, for how can we put one person's preferences ahead of another's?

This is obviously problematic. If relativism is to have any support, it must come from more sophisticated arguments. These more sophisticated arguments are to be found in legal, cultural, and historical relativism. In these forms of relativism, the argument is not that everything is relative to particular individuals, but instead that there are standards of value that are non-arbitrary, and that these standards can be derived from the law, from culture, or from history. Value judgments are thus not completely relative; they are just somewhat relative. Let us then consider whether these attempts to hold to a seemingly limited form of relativism make sense.

Legal Relativism

One type of argument that is commonly used to justify the notion that there is a non-arbitrary standard of value, and hence a way of making objectively correct value judgments about morality, is to look to the legal system to provide a standard. What is just or moral is what the law says. When it comes to deciding what is valuable in our private lives, that is subjective. But when we ask what is to be held valuable by everyone, we have the law to tell us. Hence, we know that it is right to value individual rights and equality because they are values embodied in our legal system and in our constitution. They are "fundamental values" of our legal-political order.

We need consider this argument for only a moment to realize that it confronts us with a paradox. If justice is what the law says, what is one to make of the idea of an immoral or unjust law? Saying that a thing is moral just because it is supported by the law is tantamount to saying that an unjust law is a contradiction in terms. Yet we all know that laws can be either just or unjust, moral or immoral, and fair or unfair. Clearly the standard we use first to make (and then to reform) the laws is not itself simply a creation of the laws.

Secondly, we also recognize that justice requires that we make exceptions to the law. How could such exceptions be just if the laws are what define justice, for the laws do not set down the conditions for exceptions. In sum, it seems that the laws depend upon an idea of justice or morality that serves as their foundation. To say that law produces justice and morality puts the cart before the horse.

Perhaps one would respond to this point by arguing that a law is just if the people have agreed to it. In other words, just laws are the product of popular consent. But we know that popular consent is not the same as unanimous consent, and that it is impractical to require the latter. The problem, then, is that laws that embody the will of a mere majority may be unjust. Think, for instance, of a case in which a majority of whites passes a law disenfranchising a minority of non-whites. This makes it clear that democratic consent is not sufficient to guarantee the justice of the law.

One could go on in such a vein, showing how internally contradictory is the idea that the law is what defines justice. In reality it is the other way around, for we always intend to design a "just legal system." And there are more perplexing complications when we view this idea in relation to other legal systems. How, for example, does international law fit in? And how are we to settle disputes between conflicting legal systems? If it is legal to treat women as slaves in one place, does that make it just or moral that it be done? Or do we not think that the laws of that place are in need of reform? Our "objective" legal standard seems to be quickly transformed into a relative cultural standard. Legal relativism inevitably depends on its more sophisticated cousin, cultural relativism.

Cultural Relativism

The argument one most often hears about the relationship between culture and judgments of value can be stated simply: our value judgments are based on the views of our society or culture. The well-known anthropologist Ruth Benedict expressed this view nicely:

> No man ever looks at the world with pristine eyes. He sees it edited by a definite set of customs and institutions and ways of thinking. Even in his philosophical probings he cannot go behind these stereotypes; his very concepts of the true and the false will have reference to his particular traditional customs.[5]

It is not, then, that our opinions can have no objective validity, but that they are valid only in relation to the customs and opinions of our society. Values are thus relative, but relative to particular cultures. Our value judgments are based on our cultural experience, which is in turn "interpreted by each individual in terms of his own enculturation."[6] In a culture like ours, for example, it is wrong to beat small children. But there have been, and perhaps still are, cultures where healthy doses of corporal punishment are the norm. In such a culture, it would not be immoral to beat one's child.

The concepts of "socialization" and "enculturation" serve as the foundation for modern sociology and anthropology. These social sciences are, at their best, attempts to reveal the extent to which our opinions, attitudes, sentiments and passions have been instilled in us by our society and culture. The recognition of this fact can help to free us from the conformism that goes along with the passive acceptance of, or dogmatic adherence to, the orthodoxies of our age. In other words, it is this very recognition that Plato was talking about as the first step to the liberation from the cave.

It stands to reason that human beings are, to a great extent, products of their society and culture. This insight is an aspect of human reality discovered long ago. When the Greek historian Herodotus wrote his *Histories* in the 5th Century B.C., he made the following observation:

> If one were to propose ordering all human beings to pick out the finest of all the laws, after considering them, each would choose his own: so much does each think his own laws to be the finest....[7]

Plato, Herodotus, and others of the Greek philosophers were all well aware that human beings are indelibly stamped by the opinions, moral sentiments and tastes of their own society or culture, and that they would almost always adhere dogmatically to those ideas. Human beings everywhere and always tend to assume that their own ways are the right ways, and that these ways are by no means arbitrary but in accordance with the natural or divine order of the world. By extension, human beings also tend to assume that the ways of other societies and cultures are wrong to the extent that those ways differ from their own. This is the phenomenon that today goes by the name of "ethnocentrism." Ethnocentrism is nothing more than prejudice and, in the final analysis, no reasonable person will defend it. Nonetheless, it seems deeply rooted in the bias we have to prefer our own – our own parents, children, familial relations, country, customs, political regime, religion, and so on.

Now for thinkers like Herodotus or Plato, the insight that human beings are capable of living in a great variety of different ways immediately raises the question of the rightness of their own way. And once that question is raised, it becomes obvious that one cannot evaluate one's own culture by its own standards. It thus becomes necessary to find a standard for judging all cultures that is objective, that transcends any particular culture. The "insight" discovered by anthropology thus leads to philosophy, the quest for standards of what is right for human beings simply, regardless of culture. In other words, to be confronted by the grand spectacle of diverse human cultures and ways of life leads one to discover the overarching question of humanity: how do I judge which life is best? Traditionally, then, it was thought that the overcoming of ethnocentrism required liberal education, an education that seeks to discover a transcultural perspective on human existence.

What separates the traditional view from the view of today's cultural relativist is that the cultural relativist claims that there are no discoverable rational standards for judging different cultures. Thinkers like Plato, Locke, or Marx may have thought that they were discovering objective, transcultural standards, but in this they deluded themselves. According to the cultural relativist, because one can never escape one's own culture, any standards one might use to evaluate other cultures are necessarily ethnocentric. This means that to judge another culture in light of Platonic, Lockean, or Marxist standards is to engage in what is called "cultural imperialism," the forcing of our values on other cultures.

Let us consider this argument point by point. It is unquestionably true that human beings are capable of living in a great variety of different ways, and that the cultural diversity of human beings is indeed spectacular. But how does the argument that there is no universal permanent standard for judging which way of life is best for human beings logically follow from the fact that there is a great diversity of possible ways of life? The fact that there are many alternatives does not in and of itself preclude the possibility that one alternative is superior. Consider the following example: scientists might disagree whether there is in fact a tenth planet at the outer reaches of our solar system; but the mere fact that they disagree says nothing about the truth of the matter. The actual existence of a tenth planet in no way depends upon what the scientists believe. In other words, the diversity of opinions about a particular natural phenomenon does not preclude the possibility that one theory will eventually be shown superior to others. The same logic applies to the diversity of views as to how human beings ought to live. The fact that there is a great diversity of cultures says nothing about whether there is some universal standard or transcultural perspective for judging all cultures.

Now we can consider the next part of this argument: because one cannot judge whether some cultures are superior to others, one must therefore not impose one's own culture on another. But why not? Let us suppose that my culture is particularly warlike, and that your neighbouring culture is quite pacific. If I adopt the outlook of cultural relativism, I will recognize that our cultures cannot be judged by any universal standard. I will judge my culture as valuable because it is warlike and yours as worthless because it is pacific. Does it seem likely that I will then refrain from conquering you? The argument that "we ought not to force our values on other cultures" has no necessary logical connection with the idea that each culture has its own unique perspective. For my "unique perspective" may be one that entails conquest and not peace, love and understanding. Without some non-relative standard for judging my "cultural perspective" one lacks the basis for any moral or philosophical argument against imperialism, be it cultural or otherwise.[8]

At the heart of the matter is the idea put forward by Benedict that no one can ever escape the cultural stereotypes he or she uses to make sense of the world. We see the world the way we do because we have been taught to see it that way, and not because that is the way things are. Our "reality" is a construction of our society or culture, one interpretation among many.

This argument is open to a powerful objection. To explain why a person holds a particular view says nothing at all about the truth or falsity of the view. People might believe that the earth is round merely because they accept the authoritative opinion of their society. That does not change the fact that the earth is round. The truth or falsity of any opinion does not depend on the sociological or psychological factors which lead a person to hold that opinion. Those factors may tell you something about the person; they tell you nothing about the truth or falsity of the opinion. By the same reasoning, the fact that most people believe the things they do because they view the world through the lens of their own culture does not necessarily mean that the views that constitute that culture are false.

Having said all this, one is still likely to encounter the following objection: even after the most careful philosophical probings and rigorous self-criticism, one can never get beyond or outside of one's own cultural outlook. As Benedict put it, "his very concepts of the true and the false will have reference to his particular traditional customs." The question that immediately comes to mind is this: how does Benedict *know* this is true? In order to *know* this, one would have to possess an accurate philosophical account of the nature and limits of reason, thus demonstrating that certain things cannot be known by human beings. Moreover, one needs to ask whether Benedict's assertion is not self-contradictory. For is it not possible that the assertion that one cannot overcome one's own cultural perspective perhaps merely a part of her own cultural perspective that she has not herself overcome?

These objections certainly do not amount to a refutation of cultural relativism. They are intended merely to awaken a healthy scepticism, one that will promote learning as opposed to passive acceptance of one of the orthodoxies of our age. And there are good reasons to want to be sceptical. The political implications of cultural relativism, once they are properly thought through, are unpalatable for those raised to believe that liberty, equality, and human rights are just political principles. For what are we supposed to think when the violation of human rights (for instance, forcing girls to undergo "female circumcision") is a deeply embedded aspect of a particular culture? Do we not argue that all cultures should be encouraged to respect human rights? And what are we to say to those who violate human rights when they respond that the idea of human rights is merely a cultural expression of Western civilization and has no more validity than the ideas of any other culture? It is clear that we believe that some ideas, human rights among them, are ideas that transcend our culture and hence are applicable to all cultures. It is difficult to maintain a belief in human rights and at the same time be a cultural relativist.

Historical Relativism

Historical relativism (or "historicism") bears many obvious similarities to cultural relativism. Like the cultural relativist, the historicist begins by reflecting on the great diversity of opinion in the world, only in this case, the source of the diversity is history rather than culture (in one age, Western Europeans believe in monarchy; in another they are democrats). And like the cultural relativist, the historicist jumps from the observation of diversity to the conclusion that all thought must be a product of its environment – in this case, its historical environment.

It is in the writings of thinkers like Hegel, Marx, and Heidegger that we find the philosophical groundwork for contemporary historical relativism. The historical relativist argues that there is no fixed human nature and that human beings cannot be understood apart from their historical context. This means that human nature cannot serve as a standard of what is right or proper. There is no "natural order" to the world that can be discovered by human reason and provide a permanent model for human existence.

Yet most historicists do not argue that there is no right or wrong. They affirm that there are indeed binding standards for human conduct, but they believe that those standards come from history rather than from nature or from divine revelation. This is the kind of historicism fostered by thinkers like Hegel and Marx. Both taught that transcendent or timeless standards of justice could be discovered by studying the direction of "the historical process." Through such study we could uncover the standards by which to measure human progress. In Hegel's case, history was thought to be progressing towards complete human freedom; in Marx's towards the universal classless society.

Progressive historicists like Hegel and Marx argued that history was not just a sequence of random events. Both Hegel and Marx thought there was an underlying purpose or direction to history. Hegel saw world history in all its forms – political, intellectual, religious, artistic – as a long, sometimes unconscious struggle for legal equality and political liberty. The triumph of the principles of liberty and equality in the French Revolution meant that this great struggle had finished, that history was in a sense over. Hegel therefore concluded that liberty and equality were principles that "transcend" all history, and should therefore be accepted by us as true.

Marx retained Hegel's basic framework, but disagreed with Hegel's particular interpretation of the historical process. Marx argued that history was actually a process of economic struggle, a struggle that was building up to a final all-out war between owners and workers, (or capitalists and proletarians). Marx thought it inevitable that this war would be won by the workers, who would put a decisive end to all economic struggle by introducing socialism – the abolition of private property and economic classes. The principles of socialism were thus for Marx *true* principles because they constituted the final resolution of all the tensions that had been driving the world's historical process forward.

For thinkers like Hegel and Marx, history was the means to uncovering the universal, timeless truth about human existence. Without such a transcendent truth, we have no standard we can use to say that history is indeed progressing rather than regressing, and that the historical process has any meaning at all.

Later historicist thinkers dismissed the claim that history has a meaning, a purpose, or a specific direction as naive, wishful thinking. For Martin Heidegger, the most important of the "radical" historicists, history is in fact a random process. This means that there are no transcendentally (or permanently) true principles to guide human action. The best we can do is to embrace the guiding principles of our own age. We accept them not because they are "true," but because they are ours, our fate.

This means that for the radical historicist, each period will have its own truths which are "valid" for that period, but not valid simply. Take slavery as an example. Western civilization condoned slavery from classical antiquity until relatively recent times. We, on the other hand, as liberal democrats, believe slavery is wrong. For the radical historicist, this means that slavery is in fact wrong today; but it is not wrong simply. The radical historicist would insist that it is wrong to blame an individual in ancient Greece for having slaves. The fact that

Greek society thought slavery just means that slavery was indeed just – for that time.

How persuasive is this? When the radical historicists say you cannot blame an ancient Greek for practising slavery, they assume that it would have been impossible for that ancient Greek, because of the beliefs of his time, to conceive that slavery might be unjust. Yet Aristotle tells us very clearly in Book I of *The Politics* that there were a number of Greeks who did in fact believe that slavery was wrong. Does that not make it difficult to affirm that slavery was acceptable "for that time?" Would it not be more reasonable to say that the Greeks who practised slavery were in fact unjust? The fact that "everyone else was doing it" might excuse individual slave-owners to some extent, but how does that fact make slavery right? Would it not be more sensible to conclude either that there were a lot of unjust people in ancient Greece or that Greek political culture was in this respect unjust?

A thorough consideration of the main tenets of historicism would involve a careful study of the philosophical arguments put forward by Hegel, Marx, Heidegger and others. Our concern here is to encourage you to do precisely that. For historical relativism is perhaps the single most important idol of our cave. One can begin examining it by thinking about one simple question. Is the historical insight – "all thought is a product of history" – an absolute truth or simply relative to one historical epoch, namely ours? If it is merely relative to our epoch (and it is worth pointing out that no one ever advanced this idea in any other epoch) then it cannot be true for other epochs, and hence, cannot be a universally and permanently true theory. On the other hand, it is hard to maintain that historicism is a permanent truth when the whole point of the doctrine is to deny that there are permanent truths. When you think about it, the very idea of historicism is highly paradoxical.

Nihilism

At the very end of the road of relativism, one encounters those who argue that there is no truth whatsoever. This is the view known as "nihilism." Nihilism is literally the belief in *nihil* – Latin for "nothing." The nihilist believes that there is no meaning to life, that there is no such thing as God or morality, and that there are no just principles to guide social, economic, or political life. Human beings *appear* to be different from other animals because we have developed moral codes. But the nihilist claims that these codes are all artificial, and thus, false. By nature, human beings are as free to follow their instinctual drives as any other animal. Morality is a tool that societies create to protect themselves, and through elaborate processes of socialization, human beings are brainwashed into thinking that these moralities are true. But according to the nihilist, belief in any morality is, in the final analysis, a delusion.

Few people have had the opportunity to meet a real nihilist, let alone have a discussion with one. If you wanted a better picture of what this sort of nihilism means, we recommend that you read a short novel by Jack London titled *The Sea Wolf*. This novel is about a sailor named Wolf Larsen, the captain of a sealing boat. Larsen is an exceptionally powerful man who runs his ship in a cruel and tyrannical fashion. The surprising thing is that this cruel tyrant is not only very intelligent but very well-read. His cruel behaviour turns out to be grounded in his study of natural science and philosophy. Larsen's studies, and his reflections on the world around him, have turned him into a nihilist. He believes that all morality is a sham and that by nature human beings are completely selfish seekers of power. This is why he spends his life as a captain of a small sailing vessel. On the high seas, where the artificial morality of society cannot touch him, he can rule over his sailors in the way nature meant for the strong to rule over the weak.

Larsen's view of the world is a frightening one. If he is right about life, almost everything that we take seriously – love, family, friendship – would have to be abandoned. But this does not mean that Larsen's view is false. Indeed, precisely because the adoption of Larsen's views would have a dramatic impact on the way we live, those seeking a liberal education should consider them carefully.

The question we would like to raise here, though, is the relation between nihilism and value relativism. The similarity between them is obvious: each of these doctrines claims that there is no such thing as objective moral truth. The difference between them is that nihilism sticks to this claim consistently while relativism tries to find moral truth in the opinions of the individual (perspectivism and emotivism) or in the standards set by our laws, our culture, or our history (legal, cultural, and historical relativism). Relativism thus comes to light as a kind of half-way house between the Socratic view (the search for truth) and the nihilist view (there is no truth).

The question, of course, is whether this half-way position makes any sense. Though Wolf Larsen and Socrates would have major disagreements on a number of fundamental questions, they would likely agree on this: the relativist attempt to deny there is truth, and yet to derive truth from culture, history, or individual emotions is like trying to have your cake and eat it too. If, as Larsen claims, there is no true morality, then *all* existing moralities are fictional. Relativism accepts this claim, but then turns around and asks us to take these fictional moralities seriously. But if they are fictional, don't we have to draw the conclusion that Larsen does? Don't we have to say that there is no morality and that is that?

A famous scholar once referred to value relativism as "nihilism, American-style." By this, he meant to suggest that value relativism is like nihilism with a happy ending. *There is no meaning to life*, we say, *and there is no morality. But that's o.k. – we'll make up our own!* The problem, however, is this: if we know that our moral views are made up, why should we take them seriously?

To some extent, the appeal of relativism is based on a nagging doubt that maybe the nihilists are right. Maybe there is no such thing as morality. Maybe human beings really are nothing more than a bunch of chemicals. But relativism is a strange combination of admitting that the nihilist thesis is true and then running away from its consequences. We believe that the nihilist thesis needs to be taken seriously. But serious consideration of the thesis means looking it in the eye, not hiding our faces under the pillow and wishing it would go away. Oddly enough, though relativists claim there is no truth, their doctrine prevents us from taking that claim seriously.

Relativism and the Modern Cave

Value relativism is an idea that is fatal to liberal education. We have defined liberal education as the quest for answers to life's great questions. Relativism, however, makes that quest pointless. Perspectivism and emotivism tell us that truth is whatever individuals feel it is. Legal, cultural, and historical relativism tell us that truth is relative to our laws, our culture, or our age. In one way or another, then, all relativists deny that there is any truth beyond what we already believe. This means there is no rational basis from which we might criticize either our personal "values" or those of our cave. Value relativism thus turns out to be an elaborate justification for sticking with our existing prejudices. And this explains why it is so popular: relativism seems to allow us to dismiss views we don't like (on the grounds that there is no truth) and yet, at the same time, to cling arbitrarily to whatever views we do like.

Value relativism, in its various forms, is perhaps the most influential idea of our time. Is it an idea that we have adopted freely, after careful consideration, or is it perhaps just a shadow in our cave, a prejudice of contemporary culture?

One good way of determining how free your thinking really is to check your understanding of the alternatives to your position. Socrates suggested that when people are prisoners in some cave, they have a tendency to dismiss as absurd the most serious alternatives to what they think, precisely because they have no understanding of what the alternatives are. In our experience, this is exactly what has happened in the case of value relativism. Its influence in our society is so great that it has made us utterly ignorant of any serious alternative.

Students are now so imbued with the ideas of value relativism that the only alternative to those ideas they can imagine is something like religious fanaticism. They assume that those who are not relativists must be moral "absolutists" who think they know the truth about everything and want to force their opinions on everyone else, as certain religious fundamentalists do.

The poverty of understanding implicit in this dichotomy is appalling. To think that our options are limited to a choice between relativism and fanaticism is to display a remarkable ignorance of what is arguably the most significant element in Western civilization, its philosophic tradition. Socrates, who may be taken to epitomize that tradition, was certainly no fanatic, for he claimed that the only thing he knew was that he knew nothing. Yet Socrates was not a relativist; precisely because he was aware of his own ignorance, he devoted his entire life to the pursuit of truth.

Socrates' comprehension of his own ignorance marked the beginning of the philosophic tradition, a tradition which couples healthy scepticism toward established opinion with a deeply-rooted desire to search for the truth. Socrates knew that the truth would always be elusive. Yet he recognized that it would be folly to abandon the search merely because it was difficult.

For even if it was difficult to arrive at "final" answers, it would always be possible to move from less to more satisfactory positions by testing our opinions before the bar of reason. Silly or contradictory opinions could be exposed as such. And the consequences or implications of the serious alternatives could be understood with greater clarity. This testing, according to Socrates, would bring true liberation of the mind.

The value relativists deny that any such liberation is possible. And it may be that they are right. But have you really thought this through for yourself? Moreover, if you really believe that there can be no truth about moral, political, and aesthetic matters, just what do you think you are going to learn in your arts courses?

What we have tried to do in this chapter is to introduce you to some arguments that should make you sceptical about the claims most often advanced by relativists. The arguments presented here do not constitute a decisive philosophical refutation of relativism; they are not intended to. The point is simply to suggest that we need to approach relativism as a question and not as an article of faith or a dogmatic creed.

To approach relativism in this sceptical way, you will have to go back and refute each one of the criticisms of relativism sketched above. If you simply turn your back on them, forget them, and walk away, you are really just settling back into your comfy chair, content with your chains, and calling to the puppet-master "more shadows, please."

Probably the most important point to reflect on is the question of the impact value relativism might have on your soul or character. C.S. Lewis argued that relativism has a profound effect on who we are, how we live, and whether we will be happy or unhappy. Lewis claimed that relativism creates "men without chests." By this, he meant that relativism would rob people of any real convictions; after all, how can you really believe deeply in something when "there is no truth," when "all values are relative," and when "all opinions are equal?"

Lewis thought that moral relativism would rob people of their courage (why fight for anything if "it's all relative") and of any real sense of purpose in life. Though life should be rich, noble, exciting, and grand, under the influence of relativism it becomes empty, pale, and hollow. We feed ourselves, take care of our bodies, and devote ourselves to the satisfaction of basic physical desires, like any other animal. But there is nothing human in that kind of existence. That is why Lewis called his book on relativism *The Abolition of Man.*

If Lewis' remarks ring true to you, you will begin to appreciate our basic argument about liberal education. Human beings live in caves (or what we now call cultures) and these caves have a decisive influence on who they are and how they will live. Relativism is one of the most powerful features of our cave. You probably never chose to be a relativist, but relativism has captured your mind all the same. If you are interested in understanding who you are and how much you are a product of our particular culture/cave, you cannot escape serious reflection on the problem of relativism. Such reflection would be the first step in a modern liberal education.

Chapter III

Specialized, Democratized, and Politicized: The Relativist Curriculum of the Modern University

If value relativism is true, then liberal education is impossible. We have defined liberal education as the quest for true answers to the fundamental questions of human existence. Value relativism suggests that there is no such thing as truth. For value relativists, then, the quest for truth is necessarily an exercise in futility.

This conclusion leaves us with an important question: if relativists deny the possibility of liberal education in the traditional sense of the term, what kind of education do they offer in its place? What are the guiding principles of the relativists' B.A. curriculum?

In the contemporary university, three great trends have emerged to fill the vacuum created by the relativist attack on liberal education – specialization, politicization, and democratization. In this chapter, we explain what these trends are and how they are rooted in the theories of relativism. In doing so, we hope to give you a better understanding of what is going on at our colleges and universities and why. This should enable those of you who seek a liberal education to make more informed choices about your course of study.

Specialization

You know already from Chapter I that a liberal education is intended to encourage a well-rounded and synoptic understanding of the world at large and, just as importantly, of one's place in it. The ideal of a liberal education thus encompasses the notion of "general education," that is, of knowing a little about a lot. But such a notion is clearly inadequate for describing liberal education. For "general education," in and of itself, would be indistinguishable from expertise in Trivial Pursuit. Liberal education means an education in the most important things: we seek wisdom and not merely knowledge. One learns about many things in so far as that knowledge is necessary for the consideration of the most important questions. This may sometimes require in-depth knowledge of specific things, knowledge that looks like that of the specialized expert.

What must be clearly understood is that liberal education is neither general education nor specialized training. It partakes of each in so far as each is necessary. It is for this reason that liberal education has been described as "knowing a little about a lot, and a lot about a little." But even this formulation is inadequate. We still require some guiding principle that will allow us to balance general education with specialized education.

In the past, this guiding principle was to be found in what were called the perennial human questions or the great problems of human existence. In stressing important books and raising perennial issues, liberal education traditionally focused on what might be called "matters of the whole" – questions that concern human life always and everywhere. This education thus had a certain architecture and synoptic quality to it. One's education was meant to fit together into a coherent whole.

It is this sense of a coherent whole, this synoptic quality, that is now missing from the liberal arts curriculum. In recent decades, the ideal of liberal education has faded from sight within the universities. Arts professors have become narrowly focused specialists who devote themselves to the mastery of a single, small area of study. As such, they are rarely adept at, or interested in, talking about the broader questions that form the core of liberal education. How did this happen?

Two factors are at work here. The first, of course, is the emergence of value relativism. If there are no universal truths, if all judgments of value are merely subjective, and hence, arbitrary, then the university can no longer claim to know what constitutes a coherent liberal education. Friedrich Nietzsche once said that where everything is of equal value, nothing is of any value. We seem to operate as though the reverse is just as true: where nothing is of value, everything is valuable. Accordingly, in the relativist curriculum of the modern university, since no area of study can be said to have objective value, all areas of study become of equal value. The university therefore no longer has any obligation to decide what its students should learn to think about. The students can be left to take whatever course of study they want, and the professors can be given the freedom to teach whatever they choose. The university surrenders itself to the principles of the free market.

This takes us to the second factor. What will the professors want to teach once they are free to teach anything? To understand why they have opted for narrowly-focused specialization, it is essential to note that university professors actually have two jobs. For the most part, professors are paid to be teachers. But professors themselves will tell you that they are also professional scholars and researchers. Indeed, it would be accurate to say that at most universities, the esteem in which professors are held by their colleagues is determined primarily by their "scholarly output." The proof of this is to be found in the hiring and promotion policies which govern their careers: with only rare exceptions, professors are hired, tenured, and promoted primarily on the basis of what they have published. "Publish or perish," they are told.

There is no necessary tension between good undergraduate teaching and scholarship. In principle, teaching and research can and should complement each other. But research becomes a threat to undergraduate teaching when the teachers/scholars decide to tailor what they teach to reflect or to facilitate their research activity. And because their research is usually highly specialized, their teaching becomes specialized as well. This is one of the things that has happened to the modern B.A. program. Its previously generalist curriculum has given way to a highly specialized one which takes its bearings from the research interests of the professors.

But why, you might ask, must research be specialized? The model for modern academic research is the natural sciences. As you probably know, in the natural sciences, there is enormous pressure to specialize. One does not become a chemist; one specializes in organic, physical, analytical, quantum, or biological chemistry. And within each of those subfields there are further divisions. The same holds true when we take the sciences and apply them in the professions. If you have a friend who is studying to be a doctor, she'll probably tell you that it's not enough just to study medicine. You've got to become a bone doctor, a plastic surgeon, or a child psychiatrist. The time of the G.P. – the general practitioner – is past. Once the G.P. would treat the whole patient; but today you're referred to a specialist. The justification for this is that there is just too much for any one doctor to know. So it's better to divide up knowledge into specialized fields and to seek the advice of a specialist. Indeed, a measure of the push towards specialization is that in most medical schools, "general practice" has itself become a specialty called "family medicine."

This same logic of specialization pervades the research activity of arts professors. A visit to the university library will show you that there are literally tons of books and articles written in each of the liberal arts disciplines. In order to "expand our knowledge of the field," the researcher must find some small corner of some subfield of one of the disciplines, master the current body of scholarly literature on that topic, and set to work on some aspect of the topic upon which no one else has yet written.

There is nothing wrong with the fact that arts professors engage in this kind of specialized research; indeed, it is a highly laudable activity. The danger to liberal education arises when professors come to see their research as more important than their teaching, or, to be more precise, when they come to think that their undergraduate teaching should be modelled on their research activity.

At the graduate level (M.A. or Ph.D.), it makes perfect sense to teach courses on the specialized topics one is researching. After all, graduate students are in some sense professors in training. The vast majority of undergraduates, however, are *not* professors in training. Yet the modern university insists on treating them as though they were. Perhaps this is because professors find it more convenient to teach courses in the specialized areas they know. Or perhaps it is because too many professors believe that the only purpose of an education is to train more researchers like themselves. Whatever the cause may be, undergraduate education is now merely a watered-down version of graduate school. B.A. programs follow the same departmental divisions as M.A. and Ph.D. programs. And within those departmental divisions, undergraduates take the same kind of specialized courses that

M.A. students do. You may, for example, see a course in political science on "The British Prime Minister" or a course in sociology entitled "White Collar Crime" or a course in literature on "Late 20th Century Science Fiction." Clearly such courses do not have you or any ideal of the liberal arts foremost in mind. They are far too specialized and far too narrow to raise the perennial questions of liberal education in any sustained way.

This problem of specialization manifests itself not only in particular courses, but also in the overall structure of the B.A. curriculum. Students are normally required to take five courses a year for four years in order to receive their degree. Yet there are few, if any, required courses for the B.A. The university community can no longer agree as to what constitutes an educated person or what defines the university as a community because relativism has destroyed the basis for such agreement. The one thing universities will demand of their students is that they do either a *major* or an *honours*, that is, that you complete a course of study in one single department consisting of anywhere between six and ten courses. In other words, thirty to fifty percent of the courses you take at university consist of specialized study in one particular department. The department will in turn have its own list of requirements for the major or honours programs. Usually these lists of requirements will obligate you to take one course from each specialized subfield of the discipline. In political science, for example, one might be required to take a course in each of the disciplines subfields: American or Canadian politics, international relations, history of political thought, comparative politics, and methodology and statistics. In English literature, you might be asked to do one course from each of the five or six major "periods" or "genres." As for the rest of your program, you are generally free to take whatever you want, provided that a certain number of your courses are done at the third or fourth year level. Given the wide range of possible specialized courses you might take, little or nothing can be done to integrate them into a coherent whole.

The result is a program that looks like an academic version of a patchwork quilt. Or to use the words of one of our colleagues, "nothing but side orders with no main dish." The university becomes the multiversity, the intellectual equivalent of a giant shopping mall. The student is supposed to shop around the academic supermarket, guided by passion or ambition, freely choosing the best bargains.

Specialization is understandably attractive for the student who is drawn to learning by a genuine love of knowledge and a desire to get at the truth. In a relativistic world, where it seems that there are no real answers to our most pressing questions, specialized scholarship seems like an oasis for the curious mind. Our longing for certainty, for genuine knowledge, can finally be satisfied here. The disciplines have criteria for what constitutes knowledge, methods for gathering and organizing facts, interpretive techniques, and scholarly traditions for evaluating scholarship. All of these things seem to impart to specialized scholarship an inherent dignity and value, and this is why scholars love doing what they do.

For the student, however, specialization is a trap. If the goal of a university education is to equip a woman or man to live life as a free and independent human being, that goal is not achieved by specialized education. One can be an uncivilized, nasty, boorish social misfit and yet be a great academic specialist. One can be enslaved to one's own passions, particularly avarice and ambition, and yet be a great academic specialist. One can be enslaved to the conventions and ideological trends of the day and yet be a great specialist. One might even argue that being illiberal in these ways is conducive to becoming a great specialist. In short, specialized scholarship and research do not constitute a liberal education.

Democratization

The modern university, as a public institution, will inevitably reflect the principles of our regime. In no regime is education more important than in the democratic regime. The regime in which people rule themselves is the one regime that necessarily requires an educated people. But democracy, like all regimes, has the tendency to push its fundamental principle to the limit. Democracy is based on the idea that all human beings are in some fundamental sense equal and hence entitled to an equal share of political rule. One person, one vote. The danger specific to the democratic regime is that it will fix its gaze on the principle of equality to the exclusion of all other principles. This danger is now being realized in the modern university.

The most obvious signs of this phenomenon have been lately much discussed and lamented: low entrance requirements and rampant grade inflation are the two most notorious. More troubling is the emergence of faddish "democratic" teaching practices. The new trend in teaching in the public schools, and more recently, in universities, is S.D.L – "student directed learning." Its champions argue that what is important is not so much "teaching" as the cultivation of learning. The "teacher's" role is not to convey or to teach something new to his or her students, but instead to play the role of a resource person or facilitator who draws out the students' opinions.

Two claims are made on behalf of the S.D.L. approach. First, it is seen as a more effective pedagogical instrument, one which develops in students the skills they need to become life-long learners. Secondly, by eliminating the elitist or hierarchical teacher-student relationship characteristic of the traditional classroom, S.D.L. provides a more democratic model for human relations. Are these claims persuasive?

On the pedagogical question, there is surely something to be said for the collaborative approach. This pedagogy is based on the eminently sensible premise that students learn best when they discover things for themselves: you may have trouble remembering the names of the various countries on a map your teacher has given you, but if you have figured out on your own how to get from the university to the bus station, you'll never forget the way.

The real question, however, is how much guidance you will need in your efforts to figure things out for yourself. In Chapter I, we suggested that the fundamental situation of human beings with respect to genuine education is best depicted in Plato's allegory of the cave. If we are right in this, it should be obvious what is wrong with simply turning the classroom over to the students: student-run discussions of what justice means, or what constitutes good literature, or whether there is a God are often nothing more than bull-sessions in which the participants argue about whether the shadow on the wall is a moose or a deer. A group of students who study ethics simply by discussing their views of contemporary moral issues will end up saying and thinking the same predictable and superficial things that any member of a "liberal-democratic, capitalist, patriarchal, technological society" would be expected to say and think. The fully democratized classroom thus turns into the very opposite of true education: pooled ignorance, and the reinforcement of prevailing prejudices.

Liberal education aims at moving us out of the cave. Yet precisely because our minds have been so powerfully enslaved by the ideas which dominate our cave, it is almost impossible for us to find our way out of it on our own. This is why the classical model of liberal education depends on the guidance and leadership of teachers. The role of the teacher, in the classical view of education, is to serve as a guide who has some sense of the limitations of our cave, and can therefore assist us in our search for a way out of it. Indeed, the importance of leadership to genuine education is evident in the very origins of the English word "educate." This term comes from the Latin verb *educere*," which means "to *lead* out." "Education" literally means *leading* people out of the cave because it is exceptionally difficult to find the way out on our own.

This is not to say that liberal education requires the student to submit passively to educational authority figures who will have them memorize carefully annotated road-maps out of the cave. On the contrary, genuine liberal education shares the S.D.L. premise that students learn best when they discover things for themselves. To see how genuine liberal education combines leadership with student discovery, it suffices to consider the practice of history's most celebrated teacher, Socrates.

Some of you may have heard of the so-called "Socratic method" of teaching, but what you have heard is probably a bad caricature. In movies about law school, for example, the Socratic method is portrayed as a ruthless process of inquisition in which the instructor mercilessly grills students to find out who has done their homework and who has not. It is true that Socrates "taught" students primarily by means of questioning them; characters in Plato's dialogues frequently complain that while Socrates constantly asks other people what they think about various subjects, he never expresses any views of his own. But Socrates' pedagogy was not at all like that of the Hollywood law professors. The term Socrates used to describe his educational activity was "dialectic," a Greek word that is perhaps best translated as "conversation." Socrates educated young people by conversing with them, asking them what they thought justice was, or courage, or friendship, and then raising critical questions about their responses. Sometimes the discussions would lead to a better, more plausible answer; sometimes they would lead to an impasse. Either way, Socrates always attempted to lead people to the discovery of their own ignorance, that they did not know what they thought they knew. For despite his refusal to take explicit positions, to reveal the "right answer," Socrates always had a very clear idea of what his students needed to give more thought to.

Properly understood, then, the pedagogy of a genuinely liberal education is one which combines student discussion and thinking with strong leadership from the teacher. Universities generally insist that those whom they hire as professors be in possession of a Ph.D., and they do so on the premise that the students will be able to profit from their teacher's greater learning. From the Socratic point of view, professors who simply turn the classroom over to the students are abdicating their responsibilities, and virtually guaranteeing that their pupils remain trapped within the cave.

What about the second claim advanced by supporters of S.D.L. – that it is good because it suppresses a teacher-student model which is elitist, hierarchical, and hence undemocratic?

To begin with, it is important to note that a certain kind of hierarchy is not necessarily inconsistent with democracy. In democracy, people are equal in the sense that we all have an equal right to vote and to run for office, no matter how wise or foolish we are. Yet even within our democratic system, we accept a certain kind of elitism: instead of choosing our officials by lottery, we elect as leaders the people we believe to be most competent. In everyday life as well, we constantly acknowledge the need for a certain kind of elitism: when we are sick, we defer to the authoritative voice of the doctor; and when our car won't start, we defer to the auto mechanic. This leaves us in a hierarchical relationship, but the "elitism" of that relationship is justified by the special technical competence of the doctor or the mechanic. The question, then, is whether the classroom is most accurately reflected in the voting analogy (equal right to one vote, no matter how wise or foolish) or in the analogy of the doctor (deference to the expert).

It is interesting that people never argue that it is unacceptably elitist for a professor of mathematics or engineering to have a pre-eminent role in math or engineering class. It is readily conceded that their technical expertise gives them the same title to lead that a doctor has over a patient. Only in the humanities and social sciences does one find complaints about the hierarchical classroom. Why would the situation here be different from mathematics or engineering?

Obviously, the assumption is that Ph.D.s in arts cannot make the same claim to expertise that Ph.D.s in mathematics can. In other words, the call for a non-hierarchical arts classroom is based on the premises of value relativism. Students should be equal to their professors because opinions in the matters covered by the B.A. curriculum are relative. This makes all opinions equally valid or invalid, those of professors and students alike.

Now as we argued above in Chapter II, the claims of value relativism are not obviously true, and must themselves be examined as part of a liberal education. Should we conclude that value relativism is true, the case against the hierarchical classroom would be very strong. In that case, however, why stop with eliminating hierarchy from the classroom? For in the absence of any possibility of truth in its fields of study, the arts classroom would itself be irrelevant. This is the dilemma in which the advocates of the democratized classroom find themselves: the arguments that suggest that professors should have no more intellectual authority than the students are ultimately arguments which imply that their subjects are not worth studying.

Politicization

Perhaps the most troubling aspect of the contemporary university is the extent to which both the institution and its intellectual disciplines have been so thoroughly politicized. The most obvious manifestation of this fact is the emergence of codes of "politically correct" speech and conduct. But these codes are merely a crude manifestation of the problem. A less evident, but more important aspect of the politicization of the university is the transformation of programs of study into vehicles for social and political change rather than the liberation of the intellect from the conventions and fashions of the day.

This development constitutes a powerful obstacle to those who seek liberal education. Liberal education is by definition an investigation of alternative understandings of important human problems. It is an education centered on open-minded questioning. The politicized university, on the other hand, assumes that it has all the right political answers, and sees its task as the dissemination and implementation of its views. Authority replaces inquiry, ideology replaces philosophy, action replaces thought, and the university begins to be transformed into something that more closely resembles a religious seminary than a community of scholars.

To be sure, the university has never been totally free of politics. But in the past, the university was committed to the ideal of scholarly objectivity and impartiality. Scholars were to pursue the truth wherever that took them. And almost everyone agreed that professors who took advantage of their status to push their own political opinions were abusing their position.

The traditional view was perhaps best stated by the founder of modern sociology, Max Weber. In his famous essay, "Science as a Vocation," Weber argued that politics is simply out of place in the classroom. Two short quotations will suffice to convey his view:

> The task of the teacher is to serve the students with his knowledge and scientific experience and not to imprint upon them his personal political views.

> The primary task of a useful teacher is to teach his students to recognize "inconvenient" facts – I mean facts that are inconvenient for their party opinions. And for every party opinion there are facts that are extremely inconvenient, for my own opinion no less than for others.[9]

Weber would thus not countenance anything that even remotely resembled what we today call "consciousness raising," let alone "political correctness." Such practices would be viewed from the traditional perspective as an abuse of the privilege of being a teacher, the actions of a "prophet or demagogue," not a scholar. In Weber's view, politicking in the classroom was simply irresponsible, and signified a lack of intellectual integrity.

On this point, we are inclined to agree with Weber. To take young minds and form them to your own political outlook is simply an abuse of the university. Nonetheless, the classroom today has been transformed from that of Weber's time. What makes the situation so different is that now the politicization of the classroom is openly practised without apology. There are individual professors, and sometimes entire departments, who have come to see politicking as their duty.

This tendency to politicize teaching is largely the result of the growing acceptance of Marx's famous dictum: "The philosophers have thus far merely interpreted the world. The point, however, is to change it."[10]

Marx argued that the life of the mind cannot be isolated from politics. His subordination of philosophy to politics was made possible by virtue of his believing that he had finally discovered the one true philosophical system, which he called "historical materialism." According to his theory, the real truths about human existence emerge from the workings of fundamental economic forces. What is important, then, is to devote oneself to the salutary transformation of those economic forces. And this is what many professors see themselves as doing. Some departments of political science or sociology explicitly state their mission to be the development of "class consciousness" among their students, so that the students will finally wake up and see that they are all victims of a capitalist society. Courses and programs whose sole purpose is to preach a particular political gospel now abound.

The Marxist position was, from the traditional perspective of liberal education, almost always rejected because of its dogmatism. Marx is essentially telling us not to waste our time thinking about the big questions, because he has already figured out the answers for us. Our task is merely to carry out his recommendations. The problem, of course, is that it is far from obvious that Marx's answers to the big questions are the right ones. Certainly Plato, Aristotle, Machiavelli, Hobbes, Locke, Rousseau, Mill, Tocqueville, and Nietzsche would deny many of Marx's "truths." And that is why serious people continue to maintain, Marx notwithstanding, that the primary task of liberal education is to interpret the world, not to change it. For we cannot know which changes are good until we have adequately reflected on the relative strengths of the various interpretations of the world. A genuine education entails looking at all of the fundamental alternatives, Marx included, without arrogantly privileging any of them. What is essential is to think these alternatives through for ourselves.

Until recently, this traditional response to the Marxist view of education has held sway in our universities. Almost everyone recognized the inherent desirability of thinking things through for themselves. Now, however, the challenge to liberal education no longer comes from old-fashioned Marxism, but from a new movement known as "postmodernism."

You may have already heard tell of some of the component parts of postmodernism: hermeneutics, semiotics, post-structuralism, and deconstruction. What unites all of these new approaches is the idea of the fundamental subjectivity of all interpretation and knowledge. Postmodernism, according to Ernest Gellner, is "hostile to the idea of unique, exclusive, objective, external, or transcendent truth. Truth is elusive, polymorphous, inward, subjective..."[11] In other words, postmodernism is a sort of new umbrella organization for all schools of relativism.

Many modern philosophers have argued that thinkers of the past were mistaken in thinking they had discovered the truth. Their mistakes were the result of not seeing how they were products of their time and place, of how human nature changes with history, and hence how all human thought must be understood in its historical or cultural context. But these modern philosophers did not think that this historical contextualism or relativism negated their own insights. Hegel, for example, argued that all previous thought was only true relative to time and place, but that his philosophy was absolutely true. He was a relativist when it came to the thought of other philosophers but not when it came to his own.

Postmodernism, on the other hand, strives for consistency in this regard (although it is not clear why a movement that denies the power of reason insists on logical consistency). It attempts to apply relativism rigorously to itself. This application leads to the following conclusion: any interpretation of the world by a thinker, a society, or a culture is only relatively true; and our interpretation of that interpretation is also purely subjective and relative. The postmodernist is thus a sort of relativist twice over. He or she will argue that there are only subjective interpretations and no genuine truths, and that this truth is itself merely a subjective interpretation.

This radical relativism is not without political consequences, and postmodernism is at least as much a political movement as a purely intellectual one. Postmodernism seeks to "deconstruct" all claims to absolute truth. It seeks to show that none of the great systems of thought were built on solid foundations. It deconstructs those foundations in order to demonstrate that every system of thought rests upon the illusion that it had a solid foundation in timeless, universal truth. Moreover, these deluded foundational claims were not merely intellectual claims; they were political claims. They supplied the basis for the use of power by a few over everyone else. The old foundationalism was the real source of human oppression, and postmodernist deconstruction provides us with our first opportunity for real human freedom.

Postmodernism's main target is reason itself. Reason has long been thought of as something universal, something that allows all human beings the same potential access to the truth. (For example, if A=B, and B=C, then A must equal C.) Liberal education consists essentially in applying this universal reason to human matters. More specifically, reason's task is to discover whether there are certain universal truths about how we should live our lives.

Postmodernism attacks the view that reason is universal, that it remains the same regardless of context, by arguing that all knowledge, including our knowledge of reason itself, is "socially constructed." This attack is essentially a new application of the doctrines of cultural or historical relativism. Traditional scholarship interpreted John Locke's assertion of a natural or human right to freedom of religion as an attempt by Locke to use reason to discover a universal principle of political life. A postmodernist, on the other hand, would argue that Locke's theory of religious toleration is merely a social construct, that it is determined by the social and political needs peculiar to the interests of those in power in Locke's time and place. The proper academic approach to such a theory is therefore not to ask whether it is true, but to "deconstruct" it by exposing the causal relationship between what the person has said and the social forces that led him or her to say it.

Postmodernism thus provides a basis for responding to the critique of Marxist pedagogy. According to the postmodernist, Marx was indeed correct to argue that debating the merits of the various interpretations of the world is a waste of time. For in principle, each of those interpretations can be exposed as an artificial construct determined by the prevailing social and political forces in the society or culture of the person who suggested it.

But if postmodernist deconstruction exposes all interpretations of the world as mere social constructs, then what does it leave us with? Is deconstruction not simply "destruction," that is, a totally negative instrument that give us no positive guidance for our lives? The postmodernists deny this charge. They suggest that implicit in the theory of deconstruction are the seeds of a positive and salutary doctrine: the doctrine of empowerment.

"Empowerment" is one of the great political buzz-words of the late twentieth century, a term that is now being used everywhere. Unions use it. Feminists use it. The Men's Movement uses it. Politicians use it. Even theologians use it. One reason it is so popular is perhaps that it is so easy to understand: empowerment simply means giving power to those who lack it. The other reason it is so popular is that it is radically egalitarian: giving power to those who have previously been excluded from it makes us all more equal in status.

The link between deconstruction and egalitarian empowerment is reasonably clear. In exposing the social and political roots of prevailing ideas, deconstruction shows how our ideas are merely instruments that serve to protect and promote the interests of those who are most powerful in our society, culture, or world. The deconstructionist exposé thus serves, if not to discredit those ideas, then at least to make them less dominant. This allows for the expression of other ideas which reflect the point of view of those in our society, culture, or world who are not powerful. To be sure, the postmodernist is not arguing that the point of view of the disempowered is "true," for their views could also, in principle, be deconstructed. But deconstruction empowers the disempowered by putting their ideas on a footing of equality with the ideas of the powerful; all ideas are equally the products of social construction, and hence, equally arbitrary and unauthoritative.

The postmodern argument is that if objective rational judgments are really nothing more than subjective arguments based on interest and power, then all judgments are inherently political. Hence, the various subject disciplines are nothing more than various kinds of politics. One thus finds new intellectual movements in many of the disciplines arguing that literature is politics, law is politics, science is politics, art is politics, and so on.

The postmodernist theories of deconstruction and empowerment have practical implications of the greatest importance. If all knowledge is socially constructed, the most important thing to know about a book is not what it says, but who wrote it. This leads to a new and highly politicized approach to the university's curriculum.

In the traditional approach to liberal education, the curriculum consists of the study of those works which provide the deepest and most provocative alternative answers to the great questions of life. In principle, it makes no difference where these works come from. They can be thousands of years old, or they can be contemporary. They can be written by men or by women, by blacks or whites, by people from Europe or by people from the Third World. It is true that in a corrupt form of classical liberal education, in which liberal education is defined as the study of Western culture, the curriculum centres on what is known as "the canon," an authoritative list of Western culture's "greatest hits." For the reasons we gave at the beginning of chapter I, however, we reject this approach to liberal education, and hence the "canon" which follows from it. We do believe that one might develop a kind of "canon" of great books; but the sole criterion for inclusion on the list would have to be the capacity of the work to speak to the great questions of liberal education.

The postmodernists take the opposite point of view. They argue that because the ideas of all books can be deconstructed, it makes little sense to try to rank them in terms of their inherent philosophical or literary worth. Given that all books are at bottom merely an expression of some particular social and political context, the important point becomes ensuring that one is reading a selection of works that is *representative* of the diversity of social and political interests. This explains why what counts is no longer what the book says, but who has written it.

This new outlook leads to a veritable revolution in undergraduate education. The advocates of liberal education might argue that a reading list for a course on politics should include Aristotle, Locke and Marx, because these three thinkers articulate three basic alternative visions of political community. In the politicized approach based on deconstructionism, however, all three of these authors would have to be seen as members of one and the same camp: dead white European males. A truly representative reading list would have to include writers who were not male, not European, not white, and presumably, not dead. The same holds true for courses in literature. In many courses today, the standard for deciding what gets read and what does not is less and less the inherent artistic merit of a work, and more and more the social and political background of its author. In general, then, the primary objective driving curriculum development is no longer the quest for the truth, but the quest for equality. Instead of seeking to make our students wise, universities are increasingly preoccupied with sensitizing them to the aspirations of various underprivileged groups.

When you think about it, it should come as no surprise that the ultimate agenda of the postmodernist curriculum is a political agenda. After all, the whole point of postmodernism is to argue that all theoretical activity is, in reality, political. Yet once one deconstructs postmodernism itself to reveal its origins in a particular political agenda, are the claims of postmodernism not as fully discredited as those of any other theory? Certainly its claims can't be shown to be universally true. That would be to appeal to the very view of reason that postmodernism tries to overcome; for to argue that it is right to deconstruct power in all times and places would be to make the kind of universally true assertion that postmodernism itself claims is impossible to make.

Moreover, if one takes postmodernist theory to its logical conclusion, we have to concede that the very political agenda which inspires the postmodern movement is just as arbitrary and contingent as the agenda of the dead, white, European males that postmodernism attacks. For one can deconstruct the ideas of human rights, gender equality, and cultural diversity just as easily as one can deconstruct the ideas of liberalism and free market economics.

In the final analysis, it is very odd that postmodernism is championed for the most part by people who seek to reform society. Like all forms of relativism, postmodernism ultimately culminates in a vindication of the status quo. For if nothing is true, and everything can be deconstructed, why should we change our current beliefs? Why trade in the prejudices we are happy with for new ones that are just as arbitrary?

It may well be that the egalitarian political agenda behind postmodernism is, in the final analysis, a good agenda. Our primary criticism is that the postmodernist view of education does not allow students the opportunity to evaluate critically either that agenda or any other. Liberal education, by virtue of its interest in justice, is necessarily concerned with political matters. By definition, a liberal education must acquaint students with the most profound alternative understandings of the theory and practice of justice. But liberal education is in principle opposed to the partisan promotion of any one particular political agenda, and to the subordination of other fields of study to the demands of political orthodoxy. And this is as it should be. For if "empowering" is what we're after, then shouldn't our first priority be to empower students to make reasonable political decisions on their own, rather than making them pawns in their professors' political intrigues?

Chapter IV

Liberal Education and the B.A. Curriculum

The widespread influence of value relativism makes it difficult to pursue a liberal education at our colleges and universities, but not impossible. There are a few institutions that offer pre-packaged academic programs designed to give you a traditional liberal education (these are usually called "The Liberal Studies Program," "The Foundation Year" or something like that). At most institutions, however, those who seek a liberal education must organize it for themselves by selecting appropriate courses from across the university curriculum. This is not easy to do, but you should be able to get a good liberal education at any college or university in Canada or the United States, provided you know what to look for.

To help you in this endeavour, let us divide the B.A. curriculum into seven general areas, and explain how each one might fit into the objectives of liberal education as we have described them. We must emphasize that in what follows we are not necessarily presenting these areas as they would present themselves. For the reasons given in Chapter III, the academic departments of the modern university are to a great extent guided by objectives other than those of liberal education – usually specialized research or social and political activism. Our intention here is to show you how to be discriminating in your efforts to put together a liberal education, how to use those departments to get the kind of education you are looking for.

Natural Science

Most students who enroll in a B.A. program will have an opportunity to take courses in the natural sciences – math, physics, chemistry, and biology. These subjects are of great importance for thinking about some of the major questions in liberal education, philosophical questions about the ultimate origins and meaning of the world around us. If, for example, modern science can provide us with a comprehensive account of the origins of the universe which explains the first cause from which everything else followed, then is there any good reason to continue to believe in religious accounts of our origins? And what of the moral codes that were based on those religions? What replaces them if natural science exposes religion to be a myth? A liberally educated human being cannot afford to be ignorant of the impact natural science has on questions like these.

Nevertheless, those who seek a liberal education must approach science courses with a great deal of caution. To put it in very simple terms, the basic problem is that since the 17th century, natural science has become less of a philosophical enterprise and more of a technological one. Undergraduate programs in the natural sciences are designed to produce people who are technical specialists, who can put the discoveries of modern science to work in our economy.

Reflection about the moral and metaphysical significance of those discoveries is not a priority in such programs.

It is imperative that students who seek a liberal education have some understanding of the first principles of natural science. The best way to achieve this is to look for a course in the history and/or philosophy of science. If the questions addressed in that course are of particular interest to you, you may wish to pursue them at greater length by enrolling in regular science courses.

Literature

Many of the great questions of liberal education turn on our view of the human soul. How one understands human happiness or love, for example, will depend on what we understand of the workings of the human soul. The study of literature is essential to a liberal education because it is arguably the best possible means of refining our understanding of the soul, of its peaks and its depths, of its longings and its frustrations, of its possibilities for goodness and happiness and its possibilities for misery and evil. Great writers of fiction are always great psychologists, and in learning from literature about humanity, we ultimately come to learn about ourselves.

We all know what jealousy is, for instance, and each of us has undoubtedly felt its sting at one time or another. It would be possible to gain some insight into the psychology of the jealous soul simply by analyzing our own sentiments of jealousy, or perhaps those of a friend or relative. In reading Shakespeare's *Othello*, however, we have an opportunity to observe a particularly revealing case of jealousy, and to reflect on it under the guidance of a writer who was a far finer analyst of the human soul than most of us could ever hope to be. Or think of Dickens' *A Tale of Two Cities*. We all know what hatred is, but in Dickens' tale, where the French peasantry's hatred for the aristocrats of the *ancien régime* and Dr. Manette's hatred for the Evrémondes serve to complement each other, the passion is presented in a manner that is at once horrifyingly powerful and uncommonly revealing.

All good literature will afford us similar insights. We learn about pride by reflecting on Austen's Elizabeth Bennet in *Pride and Prejudice* or Achebe's Okonkwo in *Things Fall Apart*; we learn about guilt and the bad conscience from Dostoevsky's *Crime and Punishment*. The serious study of good literature thus deepens our understanding of the human soul and makes us keener analysts both of our own hearts, and of those of the people around us.

Of course, it is essential to employ a certain amount of discrimination when selecting courses in literature. Some professors are more interested in reading literature for political purposes than for what it can teach us about the soul. Others will reduce the study of literature to an exercise in historical classification ("this is a fine example of the early Jacobean style..."). As long as you are reading good books, it is pretty hard to go too far wrong, but as much as possible, you should look for courses in which the professors see their main task as helping you to discover the human wisdom contained in the books you read.

The Social Sciences

In today's university, there are five academic disciplines that are referred to as social sciences: anthropology, economics, psychology, sociology, and political science. (We shall deal with the study of politics in a separate section below.) While these disciplines vary greatly in their academic interests, each shares with the others a fundamental sense of purpose. To put the matter simply, social science seeks to achieve in the human realm the kind of practical success achieved by modern, technologically-oriented natural science. This entails studying human matters with the "rigorous" methods of modern natural science – empirical studies, controlled experiments, statistical analysis – for the application of such methods can lead to important practical advances.

In principle, then, liberal education and social science are very different things. The former aims at deepening our wisdom concerning the great questions of human existence. The latter aims at discovering new techniques for solving practical problems, for making our world more efficient, more comfortable and more prosperous. This does not mean that students seeking a liberal education should ignore social science courses, but it does mean that they must be very selective when considering courses in these disciplines.

Take *psychology*, for example. The term "psychology" is derived from two ancient Greek words, *psyche*, which means "soul," and *logos*, which means "speech." Psychology is thus in principle "speech about the soul." As such, one would expect it to constitute a central element of liberal education.

As it is studied in today's university, however, academic psychology has increasingly little to do with the study of the human soul. Indeed, most professors of psychology would probably find it uncomfortable even to speak of the soul. This is because in its efforts to be more like modern natural science, today's academic psychology has been forced to drop "soft," nebulous concepts like "the soul" in order to focus on concrete things that can be studied with the "hard" methods of natural science – cognition, sense perception, or patterns of behaviour. The result is a discipline that is a kind of science of the brain rather than a science of the soul. Indeed, in most departments of psychology, the classic works in which the concept of the soul was taken seriously – works by people like Freud and Jung – are studied only at the periphery, if at all.

Modern academic psychology has been very successful in its new technological role. The research undertaken by academic psychologists has led to all sorts of discoveries that make our world a safer, healthier, and more efficient place. But students who seek a liberal education will find few psychology courses that will aid them in their quest for human wisdom.

In principle, *sociology* and *anthropology* are the two social sciences which are of most value to liberal education. You will recall that the chief obstacle to liberal education is the fact, or at least the possibility, that we live in what Plato called a "cave." This is a problem because to the extent that our thoughts are conditioned by our environment, it is next to impossible to approach the questions of liberal education with an open mind. Liberal education means liberation from the cave, but how is that liberation to take place?

Reflection on Plato's allegory suggests that for the prisoners to escape their cave, they will first of all have to comprehend that their cave **is** a cave. Common sense tells us that this will happen only when they finally see their cave from the outside, when they have some external standard in light of which they can judge it. What we need, then, is some way of getting an outside look at our own world.

Anthropology and sociology can be of value in this connection. To the extent that "the cave" is our culture, we can gain critical distance on it by looking at other cultures. This is what anthropology – the comparative study of human cultures – does. To the extent that "the cave" is our "society," sociology – the comparative study of different societies – can give us an appreciation of that fact by showing us the hidden, but powerful ways in which various aspects of our social organization determine and distort the way we understand the world around us.

Take, for example, the institution of marriage. One of the great themes of liberal education is love, and one's view of marriage will undoubtedly color the way one thinks about love. In our culture, it is widely assumed that the only natural form for marriage is the monogamous form – one partner per person. The question is whether we believe in monogamy because it really is the natural form of marriage, or whether we do not believe it to be natural merely because that happens to be the way things are done in our cave. In studying the institution of marriage in other cultures, anthropology can help us to think about questions like that.

This comparative study of other cultures and societies is subject to two limitations. One problem is that it is difficult to avoid looking at other caves from the perspective of one's own cave. You can observe all the other civilizations you like, but because you, the observer, are a member of a modern, liberal-democratic, capitalist order, your thoughts about what you are observing will tend to be the thoughts that the prisoners of that particular cave generally have. You will observe Islamic cultures and criticize the Muslims for being religious fanatics, or you will observe certain African tribes and deplore their undemocratic or sexist practices. Instead of liberating students from their prejudices, this serves only to generate a smug self-satisfaction.

The other point to keep in mind is that the comparative study of different caves, as practised in anthropology and sociology, is essentially a negative activity. It is provocative to learn that certain things we consider "natural" (monogamy, for example) are not accepted as such by people in other cultures. But the social science of anthropology is incapable of addressing the sorts of questions that are central to liberal education: is our custom better than the alternatives (polygamy, group marriages and so on)? Can one speak of "better" and "worse," or "natural" and "unnatural" in such matters?

Consideration of questions like these lies within the domain of other disciplines like literature, politics, and most notably, philosophy.

Politics

It is difficult for us to describe the study of politics at today's universities because this is a discipline which suffers from something of an identity crisis. The problem is apparent in the very name of the discipline: some universities will have a "Department of Political Science," while at others the discipline will be housed in a "Department of Politics" or a "Department of Political Studies" or even a "Department of Government."

These differences in name reflect important disagreements about the ultimate objectives of the discipline. On one extreme, there are those who want the discipline to be like the social sciences, to emphasize empirical and statistical studies of the subject matter. On the other extreme are those who deny that politics should or even can be a social "science," and who adopt an approach that treats the study of politics more like a branch of philosophy. In the middle is yet another group that sees the discipline as something like "current events," or contemporary political history.

For those who seek a liberal education, as opposed to a technical or vocational education, it is relatively easy to rank these three approaches in order of importance. The first approach, in which the study of politics imitates social (and by extension, natural) science has little relevance for liberal education. The third approach, in which the study of politics is treated as "current events" can be of value for the same reasons that the study of history is of value – the development of prudence – especially in those courses where students have an opportunity to look at political problems from a number of different perspectives.

For those seeking a liberal education, the most valuable of the three approaches to the study of political matters is the second, the philosophical approach. Here the emphasis is not on how to take public opinion polls, or on what our country's policy should be with respect to Japanese protectionism; it is rather on the perennial questions of principle that underlie political life as such, questions about the nature of war and peace, the meaning of justice and equality, and the character of the best political regime. Those who strive to be liberally educated people must give serious thought to questions such as these.

Take, as an example, the fundamental political principles of our regime. We live in a liberal democracy, and most of our fellow citizens claim to be liberal democrats. But why is democracy the best form of government? What exactly makes a democracy a *liberal* democracy? And why is a liberal democracy better than some other kind of democracy? Remarkably few people can articulate coherent answers to these questions. To the extent that we are unable to do so, however, it is impossible for us to participate responsibly in the noble task of governing ourselves; for most major political issues ultimately turn on questions of principle. It is clear, for instance, that thoughtful responses to issues like affirmative action, censorship, and even fiscal policy depend on a clear understanding of the tension between the two great principles that characterize liberal democracy, the emphasis on freedom implicit in liberalism, and the emphasis on equality that derives from the idea of democracy. Freedom and equality are often at odds with one another. When their demands conflict, which is to give way? Where do we draw the line? Without having first thought about these theoretical problems, we cannot hope to avoid injustice and folly in the practical sphere. For unless they are guided in their deliberations by carefully reasoned principles, human beings have a tendency to equate justice with the course of action that happens to coincide with their self-interest.

The philosophical study of political regimes will also contribute to liberal education in the same way that anthropology and sociology do. In Plato's allegory, the Cave is not merely culture or society; it is also our political regime. The political regime we are brought up in will do much to shape the way we see the world around us. In his famous work *Democracy in America*, Alexis de Tocqueville makes a strong argument that the democratic and aristocratic regimes give a certain twist to the way their citizens see all sorts of things – art, science, family life, history, and religion, to name just a few. If Tocqueville is right, it follows that we, as citizens of liberal democracy, need to think very carefully about the various ways in which our liberal democratic upbringing has moulded us. Are the views we hold reasonable, or do we hold them merely because we are prisoners of a liberal democratic cave? If it is the latter alternative that is true, then a philosophical examination of our regime will be an essential first step on the path out of the cave.

Religious Studies

As one of the liberal arts, religious studies does not demand that students become adherents of a particular religion. Nor does it demand that students give up their particular faith. What it requires is that students be open to the serious consideration of different religious worldviews and different accounts of the ultimate groundwork of human existence. In other words, it demands an intellectual openness to different views of the divine and to the question of the existence of God or gods.

One theologian defined religion as "that which concerns human beings ultimately." By this he meant that the world's great religions reveal ways in which human beings deal with profound questions concerning life and death, guilt and sin, in relation to an object of reverence – in most cases, a personal God. When it is done well, religious studies introduces students to what it has meant, and continues to mean for individuals and cultures to have been shaped by a vision of something transcendent.

While it is no doubt true that increasing numbers of people describe themselves as non-religious, the vast majority of people still persist in understanding themselves as Hindus, Buddhists, Christians, Sikhs, Jews, Muslims, and so on. They continue to see their religion as the key to their identity, explaining both their past and their future. Even those Westerners who purport to live in a "post-Christian" civilization implicitly acknowledge the continuing influence of Christianity as they define themselves in terms of what they once were.

Religious Studies is an important part of liberal education because it enables students to think more critically about their own religious beliefs (including the belief in atheism) and to better understand the ultimately religious roots of many of our secular opinions.

History

Of all the liberal arts, history may be the one that is most familiar to us. At the same time, however, history is an ambiguous term. What does the word *history* signify? Do we mean history as a coherent account of the past such as Gibbon's *Decline and Fall of the Roman Empire*? Or do we mean the past itself, the actual events and experiences of the human beings who were there? History obviously refers to both past human experience and to the systematic study of the past in order to understand that experience.

Why is it important to understand how human beings in the past have experienced life, how they saw they world, and why they acted in the ways they did? Why is the academic study of history important, and perhaps essential, for a liberal education? In an age in which change seems to occur at an ever increasing pace, a persuasive answer to this question is all the more necessary.

The most obvious reason is that history, as an academic subject, provides a student with the narrative context and background understanding necessary to study almost any other subject in either the humanities or social sciences. It is difficult for a student to understand contemporary Protestantism if they know nothing of Luther and the Reformation. One cannot understand Marx's *Communist Manifesto* without some minimal understanding of European history. We cannot understand the politics of our own country without knowing its history. For instance, an American student who knows nothing of Roosevelt's New Deal will be unable to understand fully the debate now taking place over the role of the state.

A second and obviously related reason for studying history is that we cannot understand the present without understanding the past. We cannot understand where we are without some understanding of where we came from and how we got here. Why, for example, is current political debate focused on massive government budget deficits and debt payments? Without understanding why governments followed the policies they did in the post-War era, we cannot understand the terms of the current political debate.

A third and even more important reason for studying history is that history is essentially the study of human action. It involves understanding why human beings acted the way they did, what their purpose was in acting in a particular way, and how they came to make the judgments they made that led them to act in particular ways. Traditionally, history has been the subject thought most useful for studying and improving human judgement, particularly political judgement. To some extent, one might find political science courses that develop this capacity; but for the most part, judgement is best acquired through the study of history, and especially political history, where you can see what choices and decisions have been made and what consequences followed from them.

Take, for example, the case of World War II. As any high school student should know, the sad story of the origins of that war is a clear lesson in the importance of standing up courageously to aggression, not only because it is right, but because when confronted by a man like Hitler, conflict is never avoided; it is merely delayed to your disadvantage. This is commonly referred to as "the lesson of Munich." Of course, lessons like these must not be oversimplified. If one fails to apply them with subtlety and discrimination, they can do more harm than good. How do we distinguish aggressors like Hitler from more innocuous figures? Was Saddam Hussein a kind of Hitler? How about the leaders of the Bosnian Serbs in the 1990s? One must study a large number of historical cases with a great deal of care in order to develop a sufficiently subtle sense of when the lesson of Munich should be invoked and when it should not. From the point of view of liberal education, the proper objective of the study of history is the acquisition of wisdom in matters like this, where the well-being of our community will depend on the quality of our practical judgment.

In studying history to this end, it is important to devote a good deal of attention to biography, to the roles played by individuals in decisive historical situations. Alexis de Tocqueville, observed that there is a tendency in modern democracies to view history too much as the product of universal and general forces, leaving too small a place for the actions of great individuals.[12] Anyone familiar with history departments in modern universities and their current emphasis on social, as opposed to political history, and their focus on the great forces, as opposed to the great figures of history, will appreciate the accuracy of this observation. This type of history is not without its importance – certainly one's practical judgment will be improved by acquiring a capacity to situate problems in a broader economic or social context. But it is in the study of how individuals confront great crises that students learn most concretely how they as individuals should react to particular problems. It is here that the students learn to discern the virtues and vices of the world-historical figures of the past. Moreover, in studying the lives of leaders like Churchill or Gandhi, students are not only shown how a prudent human being acts; they are also inspired to emulate these models. Such inspiration is essential, for we must never forget that liberal education is to some extent an education of the heart as well as an education of the mind.

Finally, there is a fourth way in which the study of history can contribute to liberal education. As the inquiry into past human experience and action, history raises a fundamental philosophical question: to what extent is the past essentially like the present, and to what extent is it wholly unique? History leads us to the philosophical question of preservation and change. What are the human things that change over time, and what remains the same? Is human nature something so malleable that it is completely shaped by the environment, and that we are all therefore "products of history?" Are there timeless and universally valid standards by which we can assess historical change and say that some kinds of change mean progress while others mean regress? Do civilizations decline or do they simply change? Can we make historical predictions?

Are there great forces of world history at work that mean that humanity will necessarily develop in a certain direction?

These questions cannot be answered by means of history, for history requires an interpretation of the past. Interpretation requires that one has already made certain philosophical assumptions about how we are to understand human experience and interpret the past. But history is essential for leading us up to these questions and preparing us to study them.

Philosophy

At the heart of liberal education is the type of investigation that goes by the general title of "philosophy." It seems that for most people, the word "philosophy" means something like a "general outlook," or an "approach." Teachers will tell you about their "philosophy" of education; parents will talk about their "philosophy" of raising children; basketball coaches will even refer to their "philosophy of defense."

Strictly speaking, however, the term "philosophy" refers to a very specific type of thinking, one which first arose in ancient Greece. The key concept in the emergence of philosophical thinking is the distinction between "nature" and "convention." "Conventions" are those ideas, beliefs or customs which are the result of human invention and agreement (for example, the practice of cutting men's hair short, or the British view that automobiles should drive on the left-hand side of the road). "Nature," on the other hand, refers to the way things are independent of human interference. By nature, all human beings have long hair.

Philosophy emerged in ancient Greece when a handful of inquisitive people began to wonder whether many of the beliefs they had been brought up with might not be mere conventions.

Is the sun really a god, or is that belief merely a convention of Greek society? And if that belief turns out to be merely conventional, then what is the true *nature* of the sun? Is it right that men should exercise political rule over women? Or should one say that that belief is merely a Greek convention, and that by nature men and women are equals? Or, alternatively, is it possible that there is no natural standard for an issue like sexual equality? Could it be that nature tells us no more about the political relations between the sexes than it does about the question of which side of the road we should drive on?

From ancient Greece to the present day, philosophical thinking has meant thinking about the nature of things. Are there natural standards to govern human conduct? Can they be discovered by human reason? If so, what are they? Because of its focus on questions like these, philosophy forms the very core of liberal education.

The study of philosophy may be divided into three parts. The first is moral philosophy, or "ethics," which is the examination of questions of good and evil, virtue and vice, and human happiness. This is the most important of the three because the questions pursued in the study of ethics correspond so closely with a number of the major themes of liberal education. Yet once you begin to study ethics seriously, you will see that serious consideration of the great questions of moral philosophy requires at least a working understanding of the other two branches of philosophy.

One of these is *metaphysics*, which may be defined as the study of the ultimate foundations of the physical and spiritual universe in which we live. Metaphysics is indispensable to ethics because philosophizing about ethical questions ultimately entails thinking about nature, and it is in the study of metaphysics that one confronts the great questions about what nature is, if it exists at all.

The other branch of philosophy is called *epistemology*, which is the science of knowing, including logic. Our examination of the great questions of liberal education will hardly be fruitful if we do not proceed logically, or if we are unable to distinguish between genuine knowledge, on the one hand, and mere opinion, or ideology on the other. Epistemology is essential to philosophy, and to liberal education in general, because it seeks to establish the foundations for determining what genuine knowledge is and how it can be pursued.

Now because we are prisoners of the cave, we need help if we are going to address the questions of philosophy in a genuinely open-minded manner. The most effective help is to be found in the classic texts of the philosophic tradition, the works of thinkers like Plato and Aristotle, Thomas Aquinas, Bacon, Hobbes and Descartes, Hegel, Kant, Marx, and Nietzsche. Anyone who seeks a genuine liberal education needs to know these works, not because they are "classics," but because in them we find the deepest and most provocative ways of looking at the great questions that constitute the core of liberal education.

In some of these books, you will discover extremely powerful challenges to the dominant opinions of our particular cave. In the works of Plato, Nietzsche, and Marx, for example, we find very provocative critiques of liberal democracy; in those of Aristotle and Aquinas, our materialist metaphysics is put to the test. On the other hand many of these books will be of use in understanding our cave because they constitute the very source of those opinions which now reign. In the works of Bacon and Descartes, the reader sees the first efforts to develop and justify modern science; in those of Hobbes, Locke and Mill, we find the arguments that created and defined political liberalism.

Works like these are liberating because they allow us to see our opinions in a highly revealing light. Keep in mind that those who first conceived the ideas that now dominate our lives were pioneers. This means that they were forced to think through the implications of their ideas, and to defend the merits of those ideas, in a way we never are. When Hobbes builds his case for a liberal political order, for example, he does so in conscious opposition to the authority of Aristotle and the classical view of politics. Hobbes' *Leviathan* thus shows in a most provocative way just what was at stake when we opted to put ourselves under the rule of a liberal political order.

The very core of liberal education, then, is the study of the great philosophical debates between intellectual giants like Plato, Nietzsche, Aquinas and Descartes. Only when you understand and apply the deepest alternative views of things can you begin to make progress in your pursuit of wisdom. A group of students who study ethics simply by discussing their views of contemporary moral issues will end up saying and thinking the same predictable and superficial things that any member of a modern liberal-democratic technological society would be expected to say and think. A student who knows Aristotle, Kant, and Nietzsche, on the other hand, will have the capacity to look at any moral problem from three radically different points of view. This is the stuff that true liberal education is made of.

Conclusion

Our account of liberal education began with a discussion of Plato's Allegory of the Cave. It is appropriate that we conclude with some final reflections on that allegory. Our argument has been based on the Platonic premise that the human condition is everywhere and always essentially the same with respect to our fundamental ignorance and want of education. We are always born into some sort of society, culture, and political regime. We are nursed on certain opinions, habituated to certain emotions, and educated in a particular way. We always begin as "products of our environment." The real question is whether we are content to be nothing more than this.

Liberal education aims at allowing us to be something more than merely "products of our environment." Its aim is to enable us to become individual human beings. Genuine individuality can be established only by our thinking through the extent to which we are nothing more than products of an environment or members of the same herd. It means the cultivation of a kind of self-knowledge where one begins to recognize one's ignorance about the most important human concerns.

Almost everyone knows that things are often not as they seem. The distinction between appearance and reality, between the world of our dreams and the world of our wakened consciousness, between what we have merely heard from others and what we have seen with our own eyes, between opinion and knowledge – this kind of distinction is one human beings are everywhere and always, in one form or another, likely to draw. And it is this distinction that is the foundation of liberal education.

The Allegory of the Cave is not completely unique in the message it conveys. The image of the movement of the mind from the darkness of ignorance to the light of knowledge is a part of everyday speech. The notion of "enlightenment" suggests precisely this movement. Similarly, people today often talk of "false consciousness," which suggests an alternative – true consciousness. In sum, the idea of education is the idea of making progress, of movement toward a goal. Maybe we shall never discover the ultimate truth, but at the very least we can move from less sound opinions to more sound ones.

This notion of education as the questioning of opinion, and the attempt to move from opinion to knowledge, is at the very heart of the idea of liberal education. And it is this distinction between opinion and knowledge that vanishes with the introduction of relativism. Relativism challenges the idea that there is such a thing as knowledge that can be distinguished from opinion. Knowledge, in the relativist view, is relative to opinion. In this respect, relativism ends up leading us to the very opposite of liberal education: it would have us gaze steadily at opinion and shun the very idea of knowledge. Such an education cannot help but collapse the distinction between politics and learning, between advocacy and critical scrutiny, between thinking "correctly" and thinking intelligently.

It is, we think, a singular mark of liberal education that it asks us to be honest about how we experience and think about life. This honesty demands being truly open – open to the *possibility* that relativism is merely a dogma of the modern cave. Liberal education also opens up an alternative, the possibility that when we attempt to think through the most difficult human problems, we are raising questions that we share in common with human beings in all times and places. It may be that the adjective "human" can ultimately signify nothing more than a collection of specific physiological characteristics. But if to be human means anything more than that, if there is anything about us that transcends the lines of time, place, gender, and race, then there is in principle a universal and timeless conversation about the meaning of our common humanity. To join in that conversation, or even to question its possibility, is to embark on the quest for liberal education.

Appendix

Getting Started

Choosing a University

For many students, the process of choosing a university is decisively influenced by factors unrelated to quality of education: Is the campus nice? Is it close to home? Can I afford the tuition? Will they accept me? Which of my friends will be going there? These questions are not unimportant, but they should not be the primary ones. We would suggest that you think carefully about what kind of program you want and what kind of university or college can provide you with it.

It is now common for magazines to publish studies ranking colleges and universities by comparing them in terms of their budgets, class sizes, the number of foreign students they attract, and a host of other statistical data. The universities and colleges in both Canada and the United States are grouped into various classifications and then ranked. These surveys are useful for providing a general overview of universities. It is generally conceded, however, that such studies tell us little or nothing about what really counts: what happens in the classroom.

For students seeking a liberal education, we would make a couple of general suggestions. First, you might on balance be better off at one of the small universities or colleges devoted specifically to the liberal arts (as opposed to the "multiversities" which teach everything from pharmacy to forest management, and which tend to be more interested in specialization and research than in liberal education). Unfortunately, while "liberal arts colleges" are common in the United States, there are only a few liberal arts universities in Canada.

You might also give some thought to the size of the institution. We have suggested that liberal education requires a teaching environment that fosters dialectic or conversation. This means looking for universities which have small class sizes in their arts courses. It also means looking for universities where you can come to know your professors. In general, these things are easier to find in the smaller universities, but one must not be too rigid on this point. One can find exceptionally devoted teachers and small, dynamic classes at even the largest of universities.

In the final analysis, however, the only real way of measuring the quality of a university's program is to look at its graduates. What you should do, whenever possible, is to try to find people who attend, or have attended, the universities you are interested in. Ask them if their university education changed anything fundamental about the way they see themselves and the world around them. Ask them if they think they are better people for having done their B.A., and if so, how. And ask them what their courses were like – were their professors interested in liberal education, or were they primarily either researchers or ideologues? Were they approachable and interested in serious conversation? Was there ample opportunity to debate and discuss, or were students simply lectured at? The answers you get will, of course, be mere snapshots of a very large and complex situation, but they may in a sense be far more revealing than pages of statistics in a magazine.

Choosing Courses

In the fourth chapter, we examined the offerings of the various departments at the university and made some general comments about how those offerings might or might not contribute to a liberal education. We recommend that in your first two years, you take as broad a selection of courses as possible. In first year, you should definitely sign up for philosophy and English or comparative literature. A course in religious studies or the history and/or philosophy of science would also be a good idea, although at many universities, such courses are taught only in second year or beyond. You should also consider taking courses in history, politics, and one of the social sciences, but examine courses from those departments very carefully; some of them will contribute little or nothing to your quest for liberal education.

Moreover, we would emphasize the importance of seeking breadth not only from a wide selection of courses, but also from choosing teachers you understand have different perspectives and approaches to their subjects. To have one professor whose approach is very traditional, another who is a self-described Marxist, a third who values critical theory, and so on, is not only useful – it is essential. You should not be in a rush to judge various scholarly approaches. It is necessary to have some experience in these approaches before you can begin to make such a judgement.

When choosing courses, it is worth talking to senior students who have taken them already and whose judgment you can trust. This is especially important when there are multiple sections of a given course, and each one is taught by a different professor. You should consider carefully whether the advice of those who recommend something merely because it is an easy grade – a "bird course" – is worth taking seriously. If you are interested merely in getting a piece of paper to put on the wall, such advice is worth following; if you want an education, it seems ridiculous.

When you make your initial shopping list of courses, be aware that course descriptions in university calendars are frequently inaccurate or outdated and will give you only a general sense of what your professor will teach. The best approach is to find the professor ahead of time and talk to him or her about the course. Ask the professor why you should take the course and what their views are on liberal education. Get a copy of the course outline.

Finally, if the word is out that there are one or two exceptional teachers on your campus, try to enroll in their courses. It is our view that taking a course from an excellent teacher can open you up to life's great questions, even if they are teaching a course you might not otherwise have chosen.

What To Look For In Class

Most universities give you a two-week trial period in which you can try courses out, dropping those you are unhappy with, and adding new ones to take their place. We strongly recommend that you take advantage of this possibility. During the first two or three classes, there are a number of questions you can ask yourself which should help you to determine whether you should stay in the course or whether you should drop it.

1. *Does the course seem to be driven by some kind of political agenda?* We would recommend that you stay away from the "prophet" posing as professor.

2. *Is the professor concentrating on obscure topics that happen to coincide with his or her research interests?* We

would recommend that you avoid these courses unless you already have a fairly well-defined program of study into which these topics fit.

3. *Does the reading list consist mainly of primary texts or is it mainly textbooks and secondary sources?* Naturally, we recommend the former. In most cases, you want to take courses in which you get to study the primary sources, especially the classic texts, for yourself. Textbooks tend to provide well digested summaries of the work of the most important authors. Unfortunately, they all too often resemble the relationship of pablum to a hearty meal.

4. *Does it seem that there will be ample opportunity for questions, discussion, and debate?* In general, it is valuable to have such opportunities. We are not saying that you have to avoid traditional lecture-style courses. But we recommend that you find out how much opportunity you will have to discuss questions with the professor in class, in tutorials or seminars, or on a one-on-one basis.

5. *How are the students evaluated?* Courses which use multiple-choice or fill-in-the-blank tests probably do not encourage the kind of critical thinking that is central to a liberal education and should be avoided.

6. *Who does the evaluation?* Some professors will actually let the other students evaluate you. These courses have "cave" written all over them. You should also steer clear of courses where your work will be evaluated by a "Teaching Assistant" (or "T.A."), although this may be hard to avoid at the bigger universities.

Questioning Your Professor

In liberal arts courses, it is essential that you get in the habit of talking to your professors. Start early. On the first day of classes (or even before classes begin, if possible) try to find out how your professors understand their role. Ask them what they think liberal education is. Ask them how the course you plan to take from them fits into the general goals of liberal education. It would also be very revealing to ask them whether they see themselves as being engaged in the pursuit of truth. This is a good way to identify both political ideologues and dogmatic relativists. (You may be surprised at the number of professors who claim there is no such thing as truth.)

In the final analysis, however, the most important question to ask is this: *Does the professor seem to be in love with his or her subject?* A good teacher is one whose relationship to you will be like that of an older and more experienced student to a younger and less experienced student. A love for the subject ensures that the teacher is still interested in learning and probably believes he or she has something to learn from talking with and teaching you. And that is essential to a good educational experience.

Notes

1. Plato, *The Republic*, Book VI. Translation is ours.

2. This is a question we borrowed from Allan Bloom's excellent book *The Closing of the American Mind*, p. 23.

3. Thomas Hobbes, *Leviathan*, Chapter 6.

4. C.S. Lewis, *The Abolition of Man*, (London: Fount Paperbacks, 1990), p. 8.

5. Ruth Benedict, *Patterns of Culture*, (Boston: Houghton Mifflin Co., 1934), p. 2.

6. M.J. Herskovits, *Cultural Relativism*, (New York: 1973), p. 15.

7. Herodotus, *Histories,* III.38.

8. It is important not to misunderstand our point here. We are not saying that cultural imperialism is right, nor are we advocating an ethnocentric outlook. In fact, we are saying the opposite: those who adopt cultural relativism as a means of fighting cultural imperialism and ethnocentrism are taking in a Trojan horse. For relativism can offer no arguments against cultural outlooks that are racist, imperialistic, and ethnocentric. A consistent cultural relativist has to admit that such cultural outlooks are as "good" as any others.

9. H. Gerth and C. Wright Mills, *From Max Weber: Essays in Sociology.* (New York: Oxford University Press, 1946), pp. 145-46.

10. Karl Marx, *Theses on Feuerbach*, #11, 1845.

11. Ernest Gellner, *Postmodernism, Reason and Religion.* (London: Routledge, 1992), p. 24.

12. Alexis de Tocqueville, *Democracy in America*, Vol. 11, Part 1, Chapter 20.